D4

BRENTWOOD
PAST

This book is dedicated with gratitude to the staff of Brentwood School who encouraged my first efforts at writing and historical research, most especially the Reverend T A Gardiner, W E Barron and P R Watkins.

The Illustrations

Most of the illustrations are reproduced by kind permission of the Essex Record Office. In this connection we should especially like to thank Richard Harris, Archive Services Manager, and his staff for their helpful co-operation.

Other illustrations were reproduced by permission of:

Roger Cline: *49, 50, 54*
Historical Publications: *22, 24, 26, 39, 40, 41, 44, 45, 48, 52, 55, 59, 60, 61, 69, 87, 95, 96, 97, 98, 99, 116, 121, 133, 134, 135, 136, 139*
National Portrait Gallery: *32, 127*
Richard Tames: *1, 2, 13, 15, 16, 23, 25, 30, 31, 53, 56, 66, 68, 74, 75, 88, 89, 92, 112, 123, 127, 129, 130, 131, 138, 143, 146, 157, 160, 162, 164*

First published 2002
by Historical Publications Ltd
32 Ellington Street, London N7 8PL
(Tel: 020 7607 1628)

ISBN 0 948667 81 8
British Library Cataloguing-in-Publication Data
A catalogue record for this book is available from the British Library

Typeset in Palatino by Historical Publications Ltd
Reproduction by Square, London EC2
Printed by Edelvives, Zaragoza, Spain

BRENTWOOD PAST

Richard Tames

HISTORICAL PUBLICATIONS

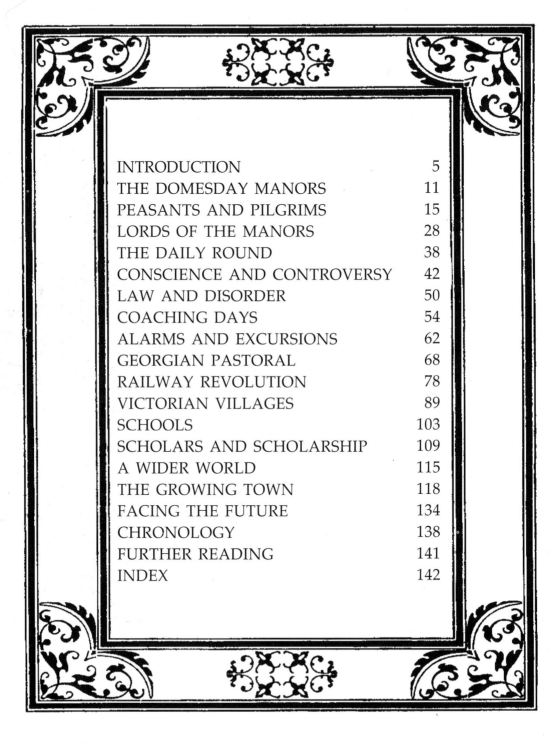

Introduction

ONE AMONG MANY

Brentwood is twinned with its namesake in Tennessee. There are other Brentwoods in California, New York and New Hampshire. There are Brentwood schools, colleges or academies in Texas, British Columbia and Long Island. Its name is also borne by a volunteer fire company in Pittsburgh and a Baptist church in Houston. These other Brentwoods, deriving their name from the original, have, no doubt, interesting histories of their own. But the original Brentwood, though increasingly suburban, has not been dull.

Modern scholarship locates the decisive battle in the Claudian conquest of Britain in AD43 at Camulodunum (i.e. Colchester), but in chapter 19 of *Claudius the God*, Robert Graves decided to place it elsewhere: "a place about twenty miles along the London-Colchester road – not a road in the Roman sense, of course – which Caractacus had been busily fortifying ... a wooded ridge called Brentwood Hill, which curved round the road in a great horseshoe, at each tip of which was a great stockaded fort, with another in the centre."

This stronghold was allegedly defended on the left by a marsh, on the right by thorn-thickened forest and in front by the deep Weald Brook. It was against this formidable obstacle that Claudius, in Graves' imaginative scenario, is supposed to have launched his legions, complete with siege-engines and even elephants, in an unstoppable diamond formation.

Brentwood may not, in reality, have been where Albion was fated to become Britannia but in 1381 it was the flashpoint of the greatest popular uprising in English history – the Peasants' Revolt. It has witnessed martyrdom and witchcraft and the anxious assembly of armed men facing the threat of invasion. It had a food riot in 1772 and an election riot in 1874. Its inhabitants endured the Black Death and Hitler's V-bombs. They have held and founded professorships, written great works of scholarship, fought in Britain's foreign wars and migrated to the ends of the earth. Many of the Puritan pioneers who sailed with the Winthrop fleet of 1630, inaugurating the 'Great Migration' of that decade, have left no record beyond their name. But identifiable migrants did include William Colborn of Brentwood, Robert

1. *Barnards House, an early 18th-century building, once the workhouse, and now a part of the boarding accommodation for Brentwood School.*

Cole of Navestock and Edward Converse and Henry and Elizabeth Howard of Shenfield.

Episodes of high drama, admittedly, have been less typical than humdrum attendance to the business of living but even that has usually been tinged with a certain graciousness. Long before so many of today's sporting heroes – Graham Gooch, Frank Bruno, Trevor Brooking and Steve Davis – chose to honour the area with their residence, it was the chosen home of the greatest Tudor composer and a naval hero second only to Nelson in fame. The area has produced no great writer but local composer Arthur H. Brown (1830-1926) wrote over a thousand hymns, most notably *O Love Divine*. Numerous eminent scholars have also lived in the locality, including William Stubbs, founder of modern historical scholarship at Oxford, who was once vicar of Blackmore.

HIGHWAY TO HISTORY

Nowadays Brentwood is a place nearly half of whose inhabitants go *from* to work elsewhere. It is also a place where residents from elsewhere go *to* in order to work for Ford or BT or Amstrad. But for most of its history Brentwood was less a place for going *from* or *to* than a place for going *through*. Much the same might be said of Ingatestone. Both lay on the Essex Great Road which, like the Dover Road, was a highway to history. In 1638 Charles I passed through Brentwood and Ingatestone on his way to meet his mother-in-law, Marie de Medici, at Chelmsford. Roundheads cantered through in pursuit of Cavaliers and on to bloody confrontation at Colchester. Samuel Pepys, as MP for Harwich, used the route regularly and stayed in the locality on more than one occasion. William and Mary

2. *(Left) History passing through – echoes of Ingatestone's past portrayed on a mural overlooking the market place.*

3. *Forever England – Blackmore c.1830.*

paused to dine in Ingatestone in 1692. Marlborough and his troops marched past on their way to death and glory at Blenheim. A decade later the establishment of the Hanoverian connection guaranteed royal traffic on a more regular basis. In 1761 plain Princess Charlotte passed through on her way from Mecklenburgh to marry George III, a man whom she had never seen and to whom she would bear fifteen children. In 1763 Boswell and Johnson headed in the opposite direction, en route to Harwich, where Boswell took ship for Holland. (Had they been a year later they might have chanced to see Gabriel Cole, a Brentwood bricklayer drink himself dead on gin in less than an hour.) In 1821 the populace for miles around lined the road in mute tribute to the passing bier of much-wronged Princess Caroline, returning to Brunswick for burial. Between the passings of the great went the passage of the many. Their traffic made Brentwood and Ingatestone bustle but it did not make them big.

RURAL RETREAT
Brentwood owes its origin to an Abbot of St Osyth but it owes its growth to its location at the junction of a pilgrimage route to Canterbury and the Essex Great Road. A town of commuters, Brentwood, or more strictly the settlements around it, has itself since Tudor times been an object of quasi-pilgrimage for week-enders seeking a rural retreat. Its rural and recreational character is attested by the local recurrence of the place name element 'Hatch', referring to a gate to control access to areas set aside for hunting. The name Brentwood itself may refer to the activities of early medieval charcoal burners.

By the eighteenth century the villages around Brentwood were much favoured by the gentry as places of recreation and retirement. A reputation for a health-giving environment attracted numerous hospitals and schools in the nineteenth century. In terms of population, however, Brentwood remained roughly on a par with Ingatestone until the advent of the railway in 1840 and less populous than South Weald until the end of Victoria's reign. Only in the twentieth century did it come to dominate the area which has been added to its jurisdiction by successive boundary enlargements. It is this larger compass which has determined the parameters of this book, unhistorical though this may be in blurring boundaries which were very real and significant to both individuals and communities in past centuries, when Navestock looked to Romford as its metropolis and Stondon Massey and Kelvedon Hatch to Ongar as theirs.

4. Weald Hall in the early twentieth century.

5. A room in an unidentified Brentwood house, with an art collection bespeaking wealth and taste.

6. Relaxing outside Jericho House, Blackmore.

7. *The Rose and Crown at South Weald. Both Messrs Ind and Coope were residents of South Weald.*

PROSPERITY VERSUS PROGRESS?

Brentwood and its environs are undeniably prosperous but prosperity has not been unmixed in its benefits. Out at Warley Ellen Willmott's remarkable creation, one of the great gardens of England, was allowed to all but disappear until its significance was belatedly recalled through the efforts of enthusiasts. Writing half a century ago the great architectural critic Professor Pevsner observed tartly that Brentwood had singularly failed to make the most of the ruins of St Thomas's chapel, which had once symbolised as well as served the town's *raison d'être* : "Brentwood could make better use of this accent in a visually not very successful town." (He did think the yard of the White Hart very fine, though.)

Brentwood's growing affluence is clearly evidenced in the advertisements which appeared in the official Town Guide of forty years ago. The seven estate agents and four builders imply a lively property market, a specialist pram shop a local baby boom, and the two travel agents, 'Photo Centre', antique shop and wine merchant disposable incomes with a goodly margin to spare. Brentwood even had its own School of Motoring.

Although the chapel ruins have been tidied up, much more of Brentwood's physical past has been swept away, particularly in the two decades after Pevsner's visit. Every old building that remains has its story to tell. The Old House in Shenfield Road, since 1973 an Arts and Community Centre, was certainly in existence by 1748 and has had separate incarnations as the Red Lion inn, the home of successive generations of the Rist family and as part of Brentwood School, the London Hospital and Post Office Telephones. At the other end of the High Street Bennet's undertakers was previously a garage and before that the site of a skating rink.

Although much has been obliterated, much remains. Local buildings listed as Grade I include Ingatestone Hall, Kelvedon Hall and Thorndon Hall, as well as the following churches – St Thomas the Apostle, Navestock, St Peter and St Paul, Stondon Massey, All Saints, East Horndon, All Saints, Doddinghurst, St Lawrence, Blackmore, St Mary the Virgin, Great Warley, St Edmund and St. Mary, Ingatestone, St Peter, Little Warley and St Giles, Mountnessing. There are over five

8. *Ingatestone Hall, the home of the Rt. Hon. Lord Petre. The Tudor hall was even larger than what survives.*

hundred other listed buildings within the juris-diction of Brentwood Council. Over twenty are public houses. There are also eighteen barns, fifteen stables and as many walls and eleven granaries. Half a dozen are other churches. There are three each of icehouses, stocks, kennels, mileposts, milestones, orangeries and telephone kiosks and two each of byres, lych gates, church-yard monuments and windmills. Single curiosi-ties include a school, a bridge, a game larder, a brewhouse, a parish lock-up, a mounting-block, a dovecote and Ingatestone's charming pseudo-Tudor railway station. The recent extension of Brentwood's town centre conservation area comes as welcome confirmation that there is still a heritage to conserve.

9. *All Saints church at Doddinghurst.*

The Domesday Manors

The future site of Brentwood lay on the route between two major centres of Roman authority. Marked by milestones, it ran from Londinium through Brook Street, up the hill, on through Shenfield and Caesaromagus (Chelmsford) to Camulodunum (Colchester). There is no evidence of significant Roman settlement along the Brook Street-Shenfield sections of this route.

South Weald, including the area which is now Brentwood, was first extensively settled by the Anglo-Saxons, as was Ingatestone, land in the Ingatestone area being held by Barking Abbey from around the mid-tenth century. The double dedication of its church, to St Edmund and St Mary, commemorates the East Saxon king martyred by the Danes and the saint to whom the Abbey itself was dedicated. In 1013 King Ethelred granted five hides of land at Horndon to one Sigered, who was described as his 'minister'. In 1062 South Weald was divided off from the manor of Havering as one of seventeen manors allocated by Earl Harold for the benefit of his new college at Waltham, which was eventually to be upgraded to an abbey in 1177. Following his defeat and death at the battle of Senlac Ridge above Hastings in 1066, Harold's mutilated body was taken to Waltham for interment.

Twenty years later victorious William of Normandy commissioned the detailed survey of his conquered kingdom which, from the relentless inquisitiveness of its compilers, became known as the Domesday book. Its compilation involved commissioners and clerks, mostly speaking Norman French as their first language, interrogating empanelled groups of villagers, speaking Anglo-Saxon, and then recording their responses in abbreviated Latin. Its successful execution was a tremendous administrative achievement, unequalled anywhere else in early medieval Europe. The information Domesday contained would be used as a standard database by government officials for centuries afterwards. As completed, the survey filled two volumes of unequal size. Essex was included in the smaller and more detailed volume, which covered England's most densely populated region, East Anglia.

Examining Domesday entries is like trying to interrogate a series of balance-sheets – potentially as significant for what they do not convey

10. *A Norman doorway at South Weald church. It bears the distinctive dog-tooth decorative pattern of the period.*

as for what they do. The apparent precision with which so much was recorded can obscure the extent of what was generally ignored – religious houses and their inhabitants, craftsmen, women and children. Churches were often omitted, sometimes even when the presence of a priest was recorded. Dependencies of large estates might be ignored. Domesday represented an attempt to record properties and their associated titles, rights, duties, charges and customs, not settlements and their residents.

Nevertheless some approximate idea of the size and social structure of communities can be gained. Some land in each was held in demesne, i.e. as a home farm, to be cultivated for the benefit of the manorial lord by servile labour in lieu of a monetary rent for their holdings. The most substantial of these cultivators were villeins, usually holding about thirty acres, the more marginal smallholders were bordars, who held land cleared at the edge of the main cultivated area or cottars, who were usually landless. On some manors there were also a few slaves; at South Weald three, at Mountnessing seven, though none on the smaller or less developed manors such as Shenfield and Doddinghurst and only forty held locally in total. Their status would disappear over the following century, largely for economic reasons. Some free tenants also survived the general redistribution of estates which followed the conquest. There were seven at Ingrave, four at East Horndon and three at Hutton, out of a local total of nineteen, plus a priest each at Navestock and Little Warley.

Domesday's county by county sections were sub-divided by landholders, running from great to less, and within each landholder's holding by the hundred into which counties were sub-divided, not by towns and villages. The core of our area lay in Chafford Hundred but other parts were in the Hundreds of Barstable (Doddinghurst, Shenfield, Hutton, Ingrave, Horndon), Ongar (Navestock, Kelvedon Hatch) and Chelmsford (Ingatestone, Fryerning, Mountnessing). Notionally the basic unit of ownership was the manor but this was not necessarily a compact or continuous estate and might include outlying sections of land, such as woodland or pasture, which were still integral to the manor's performance as an economic enterprise. A parish or village might contain several manors. A large manor might contain more than one village or physically detached hamlets which might be lumped in with the main village for accounting purposes, as at Navestock *(see below)*.

Standards of measurement are also problematic. A hide of land was supposed to be able to support a family and represented the area a standard eight-ox plough team could cultivate; but variations in the quality of land meant that this might be anything from forty acres to four hundred. Normally, it was 120. In any case the hide was used conceptually as a mode of assessing tax liability, rather than the productivity or area of land.

The basic economic strength of a manor as an economic unit could be gauged by the number of plough-teams it commanded. At the top end of the range were Navestock with fourteen and a half, Mountnessing with eleven and Abbess Warley and Ingrave with eight each, at the bottom Shenfield with one and a half and Doddinghurst with one. Most manors had at least one or two horses, though these were used for transport, rather than as draught animals, given

the lack of an effective horse-collar which would enable the animal to pull a plough or cart without choking itself to death. Most manors likewise kept a few cows, relying as much or even more on sheep and goats for their milk. Navestock with thirteen cattle, Ingrave with sixteen and Hutton with nineteen were exceptionally well endowed.

Woodland and meadow were reckoned separately. It is not clear whether the woodland was actively coppiced (i.e. systematically managed to produce wood for fencing, hurdles, implements, fuel etc.) or was simply waste, used for grazing. The fact that its extent was usually expressed in terms of its pannage value – the number of pigs it could potentially support on its acorns and beechnuts – suggests the latter. The pig was an integral element of the peasant household economy, recycling kitchen waste and otherwise unusable resources, like acorns, into meat which could be salted down or smoked for winter consumption, while also yielding hide and bone to be turned to further use or sold on to craftsmen. Most local manors seem to have had excess pannage capacity, supporting only a dozen or two dozen animals, though Ingrave had a herd of seventy-eight pigs and Hutton ninety-two.

Meadow was highly valued for producing fodder. Navestock had forty-four acres but even small areas were carefully recorded, as at South Weald, which had a mere acre and a half. In spring meadow grass provided early grazing for the sheep which yielded not only wool but milk for butter and cheese, hide which could be made into parchment and, of course, meat and bones as well. Five manors had fifty or more sheep, three a hundred or more, Abbess Warley a hundred and fifty and Ingrave a hundred and seventy-six.

Note was also made of resources found on only a minority of manors. Kelvedon Hatch had a mill. Hutton had had a fishery but it had gone out of commission. At Shenfield and Ingrave there were small herds of goats. Navestock and Hutton each had four beehives. Honey was highly valued as the only sweetener and a salve for wounds. Beeswax made the finest candles, used in churches, unlike the more common smoky, smelly variety, made from beef-tallow.

The Domesday inquisitors attempted to estimate the value of each manor as it had been just before the conquest, at the end of the reign of King Edward the Confessor and at the time of the survey. These figures provide evidence of economic expansion and contraction. Kelvedon

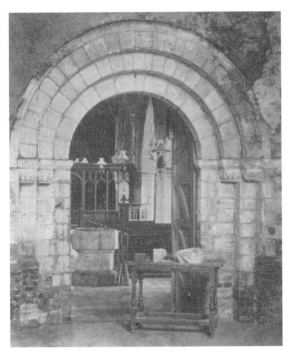

11. A Norman arch in Blackmore church. Recessing this enabled it to achieve a much wider span than usual – see Illustration 10 for comparison.

Hatch, for example, had increased in value from forty shillings to sixty. East Horndon, held by Drogo from William Peverel, had expanded considerably, from one and a half hides to three and a half hides and twenty-one acres and from four plough-teams to five and its value had increased correspondingly, from sixty shillings to a hundred. Warley Franks had increased in value from four pounds to six and Little Warley from six pounds to seven. Fryerning, by contrast, had fallen from thirty shillings to twenty.

Domesday also made careful note of changes in proprietorship, as Anglo-Saxon landholders were displaced in favour of the invaders. In 1067 Hutton, previously the property of Goti, a free man, was granted to the new religious house founded by William to mark the site of his victory, Battle Abbey. Little Warley, once held by Gyrth, was given to William bishop of London, who sublet to one Humphrey. It consisted of four hides, less fifteen acres held by a priest called Tascelin.

It was also important to record who were the actual cultivators, if distinct from the legal owner. Doddinghurst, for example, belonged to Robert, son of Carbucion, but was sublet to one Gerard.

The five and a half hides of Buttsbury belonged to Henry of Ferrers but was held by his steward. Shenfield, formerly held by a freeman, Budd, was farmed by one Roger on behalf of count Eustace of Boulogne, a magnate who held eighty Essex manors. West Horndon was held by Swein of Essex, the second largest landholder in the county, and sublet to one Siric. Landowners on such a massive scale did not scruple to acquire what were relatively speaking, penny patches. Bishop Odo of Bayeux, half-brother of the Conqueror himself, held a twenty acre patch in West Horndon, valued at a mere thirty pence, previously the property of a free man.

The Domesday situation also serves as a baseline from which subsequent changes in proprietorship can be traced. Childerditch consisted of three manors. One part had passed from defeated King Harold to the queen to the Sheriff of Surrey. Another was held by Osbern, from Swein of Essex. A further part belonged to Sasselin. By the fourteenth century a large part would be owned by Coggeshall Abbey. South Weald consisted of two manors. One, centred on what is now South Weald village, had been confirmed in the possession of the canons of Waltham Holy Cross by the victorious Conqueror, though by 1086 the aggressive Norman magnate Geoffrey de Mandeville, who also held the manor of South Ockendon, appears to have acquired half a hide of their original two hides, most likely by straightforward seizure: "but the Hundred does not know why he has it. Geoffrey says he had it by exchange".

The other South Weald manor, in the north and north-east of the parish, was known as Calcott or Caldecot. Robert Gernon, a Norman, held it as one of no less than forty-five manors that he had managed to accumulate in Essex.

Calcott, allegedly tax-free, had been held in the reign of the Confessor by a Saxon named Sprot, but the actual cultivator in 1086 was a tenant, Ralph. In the thirteenth century it was to pass into the possession of the Cistercian abbey of Stratford Langthorne, sited at what is now known simply as Stratford.

Gernon also held land around Fryerning church. That holding was to pass from him to the Montfichet family and from them in 1167-8 to the Knights of the Hospital of St John in Jerusalem. A decade later another manor, Costed, was to be granted to William of Wockendone (i.e. Ockendon) to the priory of St Osyth, which was to develop it into the hamlet of Brentwood.

To the north of South Weald lay Navestock, most of which was or became the property of St Paul's in London, though the charter the canons of the cathedral later held, stating it to have been a gift of the Conqueror on his coronation day, was a forgery. Part of Navestock had been held by two freemen, Howard and Wulfsi, as two separate manors. Valued at ten pounds, it was worth more than both South Weald manors added together. With forty-nine listed adult male inhabitants it also had twice the population of South Weald. In addition to the core settlement there were a number of subsidiary holdings. A hide and forty acres, previously held by Thurstan the Red was cultivated by two smallholders and another two hides by twelve villeins and three smallholders. A half hide and twenty acres were held by a priest, though claimed by St Paul's and another eighty acres were owned by Hamo the steward, and held by one Ralph, but were clearly marginal land, worth only fifteen shillings and without even a plough team.

North-east of Navestock lay Kelvedon Hatch. Westminster Abbey owned the two hides which were previously the property of one Alric. The compilers of the survey recorded that he had taken part in a naval battle against the Conqueror, fell ill after returning and transferred the manor to the abbey but that there was no documentation or royally approved witness to confirm this, only the testimony of one man. Another part of Kelvedon Hatch, once the property of a freeman, Algar, was held from Odo of Bayeux by the nephew of one Herbert. Ralph, sub-tenant of Hamo at Navestock, also held a hide and forty-five acres but seemingly had no livestock.

Ingatestone, held by Barking Abbey, was a more coherent settlement of three and a half hides and forty acres, but under-exploited, with only ten cultivators and a freeman. Although there was woodland for five hundred pigs it supported less than fifty beasts of all sorts. Most of neighbouring Fryerning belonged to the great accumulator, Robert Gernon and appears likewise to have had much unrealised potential, with woodland for four hundred pigs, but only four cattle, twenty-six sheep and seventeen pigs. Here the demesne farm, at twenty shillings was valued at less than sub-leased estates farmed by Ilger (twenty shillings) and William (four pounds).

Ranulf, brother of Ilger, held nine hides of Mountnessing, valued at ten pounds, and clearly run as a large-scale arable operation. Its forty-three cultivators had ten plough-teams at their disposal but while there was woodland for seven hundred pigs there were only seven cattle and sixty sheep. A further two hides at Ingrave held by the same Ranulf, was worked for a sub-tenant by nine smallholders.

Unlike Shenfield and Hutton, which had substantially a single owner, Ingrave was split up between several. The two hides belonging to Odo of Bayeux, but farmed by a son of one Thorold, were under-resourced in terms of labour and had associated woodland so huge it was measured as one and a half hides, rather than in terms of the number of pigs it could support. Another part of the same holding, added since 1066, consisted of three hides plus four acres of meadow and another one and a half hides of woodland. The hide and twenty acres of Ingrave held by Ranulf Peverel was farmed for Serlo by four smallholders.

Great Warley consisted of two manors, one known as Great Warley or Warley Magna, or Abbess Warley, belonging to the Abbess of Barking, one of only four in the kingdom to be ranked as a baroness in her own right. Other documentation shows that her tenants not only owed labour service or, later as the economy became more monetized, rental payments, but, depending on their status, they also made payments in kind, ranging from nuts to ale and geese.

One tenant owed the Abbess service as a carrier, obliged to undertake journeys on convent business on foot and carrying a pack – once annually to Chelmsford or even as far as Colchester or Ely and much more frequently into Brentwood. Other tenants were obliged to do turns of guard duty in the abbess's private prison. The other manor at Great Warley was later known as Warley Franks, being held by one Frank de Scotland in 1262. In 1086 it was held by Swein of Essex.

Large-scale displacement of previous Anglo-Saxon landowners is thus evident throughout the locality, the main beneficiaries being major religious houses and large-scale tenants-in-chief who held directly of the king himself, most notably Odo of Bayeux, Eustace of Boulogne, Ranulf Peverel, Robert Gernon and Swein, who was also sheriff of the county. Displacement at lower levels is likewise evident from the number of sub-tenants bearing French names and the increase in the number of smallholders compared with villeins. The picture of the area that emerges from Domesday is therefore one of mostly prospering settlements, scattered through an area still deeply forested and possessed of abundant resources which were yet to be awakened by the quickening hand of commerce.

Peasants and Pilgrims

HOUSE OF GOD

A sustained growth of population and the general expansion of the English economy in the century after Domesday enabled existing communities to replace, enlarge or beautify the church which was by far the largest and most impressive structure in most villages. Apart from its role in Christian worship, the church was also of central importance as a meeting-place for the management of local affairs and a refuge in times of disorder. Given the absence of building stone in Essex, the area became noted for its outstanding architectural achievements in timber and, later, brick. Professor Pevsner has praised St Lawrence, Blackmore as having "one of the most impressive, if not the most impressive, of all timber towers in England". Another outstanding example is at Navestock and there are noteworthy timber arcades at Navestock and Shenfield. Ingatestone and Fryerning churches have handsome brick towers and Blackmore a brick arcade. These striking features date from the later medieval period but there are numerous visible, if fragmentary, traces dating back to the expansive eleventh to thirteenth centuries. The oldest part of Ingatestone's parish church, the north wall, dates from the late eleventh century, as do the nave and chancel of the church at Fryerning. Fryerning's font, of Caen stone, dates from the twelfth century. St Peter and St Paul in Stondon Massey was probably begun around 1100. Timbers in the church of St Thomas the Apostle at Navestock have been dated to 1120-40. A church was known to be in existence at South Weald by about 1150. A century later the living was prosperous enough to support the rebuilding of its chancel and the addition of a north aisle. St Mary's

12. *The parish church of St Thomas the Apostle, Navestock, reproduced as a Christmas card.*

~Navestock Church, Essex~

~Best Christmas Wishes from all at Congresbury~

13. *St Lawrence church, Blackmore. The tower of this church has been praised by Nikolaus Pevsner as perhaps the most impressive in England.*

14. *The unusual late medieval timber arcading of St Mary's Shenfield.*

15. *Marygreen Manor Hotel, with a history of medieval to modern (see p.27).*

16. *The flag flying at half-mast over St Mary the Virgin, Fryerning, marks the passing of the Queen Mother in 2002.*

17. St Giles, Mountnessing, in splendid isolation.

18. A medieval depiction of Humanity and Eternity, the cycle of life, in Ingatestone's church..

at Shenfield was in existence by 1249. All Saints, Doddinghurst and St Giles at Mountnessing also date from at least the thirteenth century.

The foundation of Blackmore priory by Adam de Sandford and Jordan, chamberlains to the queen, can be dated to 1155. It was an Augustinian house, dedicated to St Lawrence, and for centuries followed the routines of monastic life uneventfully.

Another religious house, Thoby Priory, was established at Mountnessing by the 1140s. In 1262 Bartholomew Blunt of Billericay sided with the revolt led by Simon de Montfort. Following the rebels' defeat at Evesham Blunt's lands were confiscated and made over to Thoby Priory.

19. *Ruined arches at Thoby Priory recall its monastic origins.*

20. *Structural plan of the tower of St Giles, Mountnessing.*

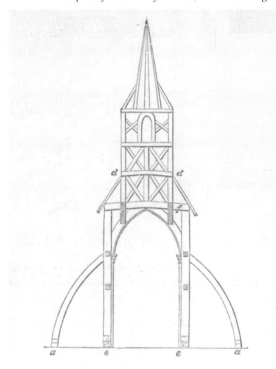

THE BEGINNINGS OF BRENTWOOD

The first recorded reference to Brentwood occurs in 1176 as the surname of one Reginald de bosco arso (of the burnt wood), a fugitive or outlaw whose goods and chattels, valued at eight shillings, were deemed to have been forfeited to the Crown. Shortly after this, between 1177 and 1184, Henry II confirmed the grant of the Brentwood estate known as Corstede, made by William of Ockendon to the newly founded (1177) Abbey of St Osyth – in return for which the donor was to receive the performance of prayers for the benefit of himself and his family. The king added to this benefaction licence to deforest and cultivate forty acres, to cut wood and to be free from the jurisdiction of the special forest courts which safeguarded royal hunting rights. From these evidences the existence of a settled community at Brentwood by the last third of the twelfth century may reasonably be inferred. It was at first probably no more than a small cluster of wood-framed houses straggling along a forest clearing created by the substantial fire – accidental or deliberate – from which Brentwood derives its name. It is to the Abbey of St Osyth, therefore, that the systematic development of Brentwood as an urban settlement must be credited. Occupying the high-

21. The medieval font at Herongate.

22. The Leper Hospital in Southwark. Most leper hospitals were more isolated than this one.

est ground in the parish of South Weald and lying at the junction of the London-Colchester road and the Ongar-Tilbury road, it was clearly chosen as a site with a potential for growth, a choice which was soon to be vindicated. Occasional royal grants of permission to assart – encroach on forest for cultivation – provide evidence of pressure of population on the land throughout the late twelfth and thirteenth centuries. Arable farming appears to have been predominant, with little pasture, except along the higher ground in the north-east of the parish.

By 1201 there was a leper hospital in existence at Brook Street, then known as Sideburgbroc – literally meaning "the brook by the wide earthwork". It was usual for such institutions to be within sight of a highway, so that itinerant sufferers could take shelter there and the pious passer-by could donate alms. It was also normal for it to be distinctly separated by distance from any significant settlement, in this case the emerging town of Brentwood a mile up the hill. A house was built for the Master of the leper hospital in 1290; part of this was later incorporated into the Golden Fleece.

1221 is the probable date for the building of a chapel dedicated to St Thomas Becket, just over half a century after the saint's martyrdom. During that period his shrine at Canterbury had become a major object of veneration, attracting a constant traffic of pilgrims. Many would have come from the eastern counties, then the most densely settled and prosperous part of the kingdom, and of those a significant number would

have passed through Brentwood en route to take ferry across the Thames at Tilbury. The name of Pilgrims' Hatch, however, is only recorded from 1483.

Permission to build the new chapel was granted to David, Abbot of St Osyth's, by the Abbot of Waltham and Richard, vicar of South Weald. The latter would have had to have been satisfied that this new establishment represented no threat to his cure of souls in the locality and presumably accepted that its primary purpose was to cater to the 'passing trade' represented by pilgrim traffic heading south and other travellers heading north into East Anglia or to take ship from Harwich. To safeguard the rights of the mother church at South Weald it was therefore explicitly laid down that the chaplain appointed to St Thomas's should not, without express leave, admit local parishioners to communion or confession, nor perform either baptisms or burials on their behalf. It was further decreed that on the feast of St Thomas or at the time of a fair, if one should be granted, the parishioners might have recourse to the chapel but that the vicar reserved the right on such occasions to perform the services or send a deputy to do so on his behalf. The chaplain was, moreover, expected to rely on the offerings of pilgrims and other strangers for his income and not to look to the parish. By 1388, however, when the chaplain was Bordinus de Depford, the Abbey of St

23. The ruins of St Thomas's chapel, Brentwood High Street.

24. Thomas Becket, depicted at the moment of his assassination.

Osyth had allocated lands for his support to the value of fifty-two shillings. In the same year Edmund of Langley, Duke of York, founded a chantry in the chapel, dedicated to St Mary, in memory of his sister, Isabel de Coucy, Countess of Bedford, who had died in 1379. A priest designated for the specific service of the chantry was presented by the duke in 1393. Why a modest chapel a day's ride from the capital should have been selected for this purpose is not self-evident, though the fact that the court of King's Bench had been convened in Brentwood in 1389 suggests that it had by then become a place of some significance.

In 1227 the right to hold at Brentwood a weekly Wednesday market and a two-day fair on the Vigil and Feast of St Thomas was granted to the Abbot and Canons of St Osyth. The market day was changed to Thursday in 1252.

In 1232 the Prior and canons of Blackmore were granted the right to hold an annual fair of their own, further evidence of the growing prosperity of the area.

It was to be held for three days starting on 9 August, the vigil before the feast of St Lawrence, to whom the priory was dedicated. In 1234 Thomas de Canville, lord of the manor of Shenfield, was granted the right to build houses along the highway on land he held in Brentwood, opposite those already built by the Abbot of St Osyth.

By 1276 Putwell (formerly Dell) bridge was in existence to carry travellers along the London-Colchester road over the Weald Brook. Responsibility for the erection and maintenance of bridges was an expensive obligation and in this case devolved upon Waltham Abbey.

Brentwood's reputation as a healthy location – in contrast to the low-lying Thames-side marshland to its south – was confirmed more than half a millennium ago. Around 1400 the Abbess of Barking ordered the construction of a sanatorium at Great Warley. It was complemented by a purpose-built pond for fish. Observant clergy would have been restricted to fish on about half the days of the year. Warley Place was later built at the same location.

25. *Late-medieval houses in Brentwood High Street, still standing in 2002.*

HIGH DRAMA IN THE HIGH STREET

In 1216 Henry III succeeded to the throne as a nine-year-old child. He was fortunate in having as regent the veteran warrior William Marshall, Earl of Pembroke, a man of total integrity, and as justiciar or chief minister the able Hubert de Burgh, who had served King John in the same capacity. Under their leadership a major baronial rebellion, aiming at putting Prince Louis of France on the throne, was suppressed by 1217. Hubert, no dry administrator but a valiant warrior, was personally responsible for destroying a French fleet bringing reinforcements in a day-long sea-fight off Dover. After William's death in 1219 Hubert became the dominant figure in government and as a matter of political conviction sought to frustrate the infiltration of foreigners into appointments he wished to reserve for Englishmen. In 1226 the king created Hubert Earl of Kent and amongst other properties granted him the manor of Warley Franks. Henry assumed the right to rule in person as king in 1227 but confirmed Hubert in office as justiciar for life in 1228.

Hubert tried repeatedly but fruitlessly to restrain the king from undertaking wasteful expeditions against France. When these ended in fiasco Hubert was blamed and, egged on by the ambitious Peter des Roches, a French rival eager to supplant de Burgh, Henry III summarily dismissed him in 1232, presenting him with a long list of allegations of abuse of office, ranging from corruption to poisoning, seduction and sorcery. Hubert, having initially taken refuge in Merton Priory, was granted an interval of respite to prepare his defence and decided to visit Bury St Edmunds where his wife was residing. En route back to London he stopped overnight at Brentwood in a house belonging to his nephew, Thomas Blundville, Bishop of Norwich. Warned of the approach of Godfrey de Gravecumb, Steward of the Royal Household, at the head of three hundred soldiers, Hubert bolted for St Thomas's chapel to claim sanctuary. Despite the fact that he was holding a cross in one hand and the Host in the other, he was unceremoniously dragged from his refuge and a smith called to fit him with fetters. Roger of Wendover, the St Albans chronicler recounting this dramatic episode, manufactured for the smith a speech which credited the humble artisan with an extraordinary grasp of English and European affairs and a commensurate gift of eloquence. On being informed of the identity of the captive the smith is alleged to have refused outright, even at risk of his own life, to fetter the fallen minister: "Is not Hubert de Burgh faithful and great hearted? Has he not often rescued England from foreigners and restored England to the English. Has he not served his master King John so constantly and faithfully in Gascony, Normandy and elsewhere that he was sometimes forced to eat his horses: so well indeed that even our enemies praised his wonderful devotion? Has he not saved Dover for us, the key to England and protected it against the King of France and his mighty power?" Carried away by his own rhetoric the smith then invoked Hubert's "great deeds at Lincoln" – a battle at which the former justiciar had not even been present – and concluded defiantly "May God judge between you and him, because you have treated him unjustly and cruelly, giving him the very worst things in return for his best." Whether the smith said any such thing, whether, indeed, there was an incident with a smith at all, one might plausibly doubt. There is much less doubt, however, that the denunciation concocted by the chronicler to put into the smith's mouth clearly represented the deep loathing and animosity felt among the politically conscious and relevant sections of English society towards the avaricious French favourites with which the young king had surrounded himself and who were to be a constant source of friction throughout his lengthy reign.

Smith or no smith, speech or no speech, Hubert was bundled off to the Tower by Godfrey – until Roger, Bishop of London learned of the blatant violation of sanctuary that had cast him there and threatened excommunication on all those who had taken part in the Brentwood fracas unless Hubert was returned to the chapel. Henry backed down and ordered Hubert's return to sanctuary but violated the spirit, at least, of his compliance by having the chapel surrounded with a close guard and forbidding any person from giving or selling the prisoner anything to eat or drink, beyond the halfpenny loaf and, admittedly large, measure of ale which constituted his official daily allowance. As the forty-day period of sanctuary drew to a close Hubert finally conceded the impossibility of his situation, surrendered voluntarily to his besiegers and was once more confined to the Tower. Having served imprisonment until 1234 for his alleged treasons, Hubert was subsequently pardoned and released to enjoy his – much diminished – estates in retirement until his death in 1243.

REVOLT!

The lay subsidy returns for 1327 listed the names of forty-nine assessable men in South Weald and Brentwood, making it by some margin the largest settlement in Chafford hundred. Payment was levied at 5% of the value of a person's movable goods and the returns reveal that the two hundreds in Essex contributing the most tax in relation to their area were Chafford and Rochford.

Within Chafford hundred, however, the riverside communities were clearly wealthier in relation to their size than the inland ones. Grays Thurrock yielded 31s 6d per square mile, South Weald and Brentwood only 10s 9d. The 1334 lay subsidy valued South Weald and Brentwood together at £117 4s 6d, putting it on a par with Witham (£118 4s 6d and well ahead of Braintree, £92 6s 3d), Chelmsford (£69 1s 10d), Ingatestone (£46s 6s 8d) and Ongar (£37 13s 4d). Such prosperity would have been severely damaged by the unprecedented epidemic of bubonic plague, known as the Black Death, which devastated Britain in 1348-9 and returned again in 1361. The isolation of the church at Buttsbury suggests a particularly virulent outbreak among the community which formerly surrounded it.

The result of the Black Death was a major reduction in the labour supply and a general dislocation of prices and markets. To this must be added the tensions generated by the Hundred Years War against France. English society, already violent by twentieth century standards, enlarged its potential for violence by increasing the numbers of men who had seen active service in France and returned brutalised and emboldened by the experience of combat and its invariable accompaniments of rapine and looting.

The long reign of Edward III (1327-77) drew to a dismal close as memories of the glorious victories of Crecy and Poitiers faded and the king slipped into senility. Nothing more vividly symbolises the weakness of royal authority than the fact that when the king at last died his corpse was stripped of its rings by his mistress Alice Perrers, who then retired to her manor of Upminster to enjoy her gains. The throne passed to ten-year-

26. *The Luttrell Psalter of c.1340 depicts an industrious idyll, shortly to be savagely disrupted by plague and the strains of war.*

old Richard of Bordeaux, under the tutelage of his uncle, John of Gaunt. The war with France still had to be paid for and in 1377 it was decided to have recourse to the novel device of a poll tax on the laity, from which only beggars and children under fifteen were exempted. The charge was a groat, four pence. The authorities imposed it again in 1379 at a rate of three groats, a week's wages for a labourer. It was imposed for a third time in 1381 at the same rate only to encounter evasion on a massive scale. Comparison of the returns of 1377 and 1381 revealed that the adult population had apparently fallen by a third. In Essex the taxable population had seemingly contracted from 46,962 to 30,748. Commissioners were ordered out into the shires to investigate the shortfall and to extort cash from recalcitrants. Thomas Bampton, Commissioner for Essex, held a court of inquiry at Brentwood on 30 May 1381, summoning a jury to represent the hundred of Barstable. In reply to questioning the men of Fobbing claimed to have a quittance acknowledging that they had paid their tax and therefore were justified in refusing to part with another penny. When Bampton, who had an escort of two men-at-arms, menaced them with a threat of punishment they successfully enlisted the support of neighbours from Corringham and Stanford-le-Hope and drove the Commissioner and his escort out of town. When no less a person than Sir Robert Belknappe, Chief Justice of the Common Pleas, was sent down to punish the evildoers, he was similarly treated, having been forced to swear that he would make no further attempt to pursue the guilty men and would divulge the informants who had been called upon to name the original rioters. Those informants that they could catch the Brentwood mob beheaded, together with three clerks. Placing their heads on pikes, the mob then surged off in search of plunder, eventually joining the swelling stream of angry men surging towards London to confront the king's ministers.

Thanks largely to the nerve of the boy king himself the government weathered the crisis – at the cost of a few prominent heads – and counterattacked over the course of the summer. A still rebellious remnant of the Essex contingent was crushed at Billericay and a special assize convened at Chelmsford on 4 July. The accused included men from South Weald, Warley, Ingrave and "Gyngattestane" (Ingatestone)"who rose up against the king and gathered congregations at Brendewood and made assault on justices of the peace with bows and arrows to kill them, afterwards they rode about armed in the land of peace and did many ill deeds."

Richard II is known to have passed through Brentwood again in 1392. His sojourn may have given the White Hart its name, because that was the badge worn by his retainers and it was during his reign that Parliament passed an Act requiring retailers of ale to put up a sign so that the aleconners could test their product for quality.

A MAN OF DISTINCTION
For an ecclesiastic of such eminence the details of the life of Edmund Coningsburgh are tantalisingly fragmentary. Neither the date of his birth nor of his death are certain. He was probably educated at Cambridge and is known to have held the rectory of St Leonard, Foster Lane in London in 1447-8. In October 1450 he became vicar of South Weald and a year later rector of Copford, near Colchester. From 1455 onwards he was much employed in Cambridge University

27. *Essex Lady – Alice Tyrrell's tomb slab in All Saints, East Horndon.*

28. *The remains of Heron Hall, as depicted c.1810.*

29. *All Saints, East Horndon. Its rebuilding was paid for by the Tyrrell family.*

affairs and later became a royal envoy from Edward IV to Pope Sixtus IV. He was rewarded with the Archbishopric of Armagh but papal opposition to this appointment made him willing to resign it for a very modest annual pension of fifty marks in 1479. Nothing more is known of his later career.

A POWERFUL FAMILY

The Tyrrells of Heron Hall claimed descent from Walter Tirel, alleged slayer of William II. Sir John Tyrrell (died 1437), who fought at Agincourt in Henry V's personal retinue, sat as MP for Essex in twelve parliaments and served as Speaker in three. He also served as sheriff of Essex and Hertfordshire. His grandson Sir James Tyrrell has the dubious distinction of being the alleged murderer of the 'Princes in the Tower', for which he was executed at Tower Hill in 1502. In the late fifteenth century the Tyrrells were responsible for the almost complete reconstruction of All Saints, East Horndon in brick. The church still contains an incised memorial slab to Lady Alice Tyrrell who died in 1422. It has been described as the finest of its kind in England.

RURAL RETREATS

An inventory of 1335 details the extent of the manorial farmhouse at Navestock, then held by Adam de Murimuth (?1275-1347), a canon of St Paul's. Murimuth was a high-flying lawyer who had been employed on royal business in Rome, Avignon and Sicily. Towards the end of his life he wrote a chronicle of the period since 1303, continuing it until the year of his death.

We may perhaps think of him as an early example of a type that was to become a significant local phenomenon in later centuries – a successful Londoner gratified to have the option of retreating to his place in the country. The main property consisted of a hall with a buttery and pantry at one end and a chamber with galleries at the other and under the same roof a bakehouse and dairy, a kitchen, a hen house, another chamber with a store room and another chamber above it and a plastered chapel. Outside there was an old four bay granary, an old kiln, a small byre for calves, a smithy, a sheepfold and a windmill.

In the early fifteenth century Sir John Fitz-Lewis, a vintner and goldsmith, built a brick mansion at West Horndon and was granted a licence to crenellate it. This was probably more an indication of his knightly rank than a serious effort at fortification. The house, however, was doomed to a frightful fate at the end of the century, being consumed by fire on the wedding-night of the merchant's grandson, who perished in the flames with his bride. A monument to Sir Richard Fitzlewes (died 1528) and his four wives can be seen in St Nicholas, Ingrave.

According to the eighteenth-century Essex historian Philip Morant, writing in 1768, the original manor house of Brizes at Kelvedon Hatch was built around 1498 by Thomas Bryce, a London mercer. In 1515 it was sold to Sir John Allen, a London alderman.

George Lloyd's lovingly-crafted history of Marygreen Manor hotel, *The Place at Brook Street*, *(see ill. 15)* traces its origins to an adjunct property of the leper hospital which once stood opposite. By the early sixteenth century it had become the country home of Henry Roper, a velvet-robed Yeoman of the Royal Bedchamber in the household of Queen Katherine of Aragon. Roper died in 1517 and the property passed to his godsons, Henry and Thomas Roper. The latter disposed of it to the Wrights of Kelvedon Hatch in 1533 but it continued to be known as the Manor of Ropers for a further two and a half centuries.

Blackmore House, in the shadow of the church of St Lawrence, served as an occasional royal residence and was jokingly known as Jericho at the court of Henry VIII on account of its supposed remoteness. According to Morant the young Henry VIII developed the habit of using it as a rural hideaway "when he had a mind to be lost with his courtesans". There the king enjoyed a liaison with Bessie Blount, a lady-in-waiting to his Spanish queen. Their offspring, Harry Fitzroy (1519-36), at six was created a Garter Knight, Duke of Richmond and Lord High Admiral and at fourteen was married to a daughter of the Duke of Norfolk. His death at seventeen has been attributed to poisoning in revenge for the slighting of Queen Katherine.

Lords of the Manors

"Whosoever ... can live without manual labour,
and thereto is able and will bear the port, charge
and countenance of a gentleman, he shall for money
have a coat of arms bestowed upon him by heralds
(who in the charter of the same do of custom
pretend antiquity and service and many gay things)
and thereunto being made so good cheap, be called
Master, which is the title that men give to esquires
and gentlemen, and reputed for a gentleman ever
after."

William Harrison – *Description of England* (1577)

Harrison, rector of Radwinter, Essex, made it
clear that a gentleman was one who was taken
for a gentleman and could play the part and bear
the costs of keeping up the outward signs of such
a status – land, a coat of arms, a dignified house,
fine clothes, open-handed hospitality and a staff
of servants required to maintain all these. The
relationship between wealth and gentle status
was real but imprecise. A certain capital and
security of income was a minimum prerequisite
but no guarantee of automatic entry into the
ranks of the gentry, much less progression to the
peerage. An Act of Parliament of 1429 had de-
fined *les gentiles* as possessors of freehold land
worth forty shillings a year or more. A century
later the term gentleman was applied to anyone
free from the need to labour, an indication,
perhaps, that an increasing number could lay
claim to the status. The expansion of the ranks
of the gentry has been attributed to several plau-
sible factors. The Tudor era was marked by a
sustained rise in population which contrasted
strongly with the stagnation of the previous
century. This depressed labourers' wages and
pushed up food prices, widening the gap between haves and have-nots. It also meant a rising
demand for agrarian products of all kinds – food,
wool, leather etc. – especially in London, which
grew significantly faster than England as a whole.
Being part of the capital's rural hinterland,
Brentwood and its environs were bound to feel
the effect. Rising inflation made borrowing
cheaper – for those with collateral – to finance
building and land deals in the buoyant market
created by royal confiscation of monastic estates
in the 1530s. This was certainly significant in the
Brentwood area, where so much land had been
in ecclesiastical hands. The good order established by the Tudors likewise fostered the con-
fidence needed to make investments. Their lavish
court encouraged luxury and ambition but also,
through service to the state, opened up huge
opportunities for self-aggrandisement. Again, this
was to prove a factor of major significance in the
Brentwood area, where the 'new men' who moved
in would range from a minor functionary in the
royal cellars to a full-fledged secretary of state.
As Felicity Heal and Clive Holmes observe in
their important survey of *The Gentry in England
and Wales 1500-1700,* in counties close to London,
such as Essex, an already mobile elite was rein-
forced by grants to courtiers and royal officials.
The openness of this elite is further evidenced by
the willingness of its members to seek marriage
partners outside its own county set. A survey of
gentry marriage-alliances as they stood on the
eve of the civil wars of the 1640s shows that in
Kent to the immediate south no less than 82%
were made within the county boundaries, in
Suffolk to the immediate north 69% but in Essex
only 43.3%.

DISSOLUTION AND ADVANCEMENT

The dispossession of the abbeys of St Osyth,
Stratford and Waltham, taken with the dissolution of local religious houses, necessarily involved
a revolution in local land-ownership.This brought
to prominence a new breed of opportunistic,
upwardly mobile, *arriviste* gentry, led locally by
the Petres and the Brownes. The process actually
began a decade before the break with Rome
because in 1525 Wolsey ordered the dissolution
of Blackmore and Thoby priories to fund his
projected educational foundations at Oxford and
Ipswich. Both Blackmore and Thoby had dwindled to relative insignificance. Blackmore, valued at around £85 a year, had only a prior and
three canons, and Thoby, valued at some £75, a
prior and two canons. The present Blackmore
church is structurally part of the nave of the
former priory, most of which was pulled down
by Sir Brian Tuke, treasurer of the royal household. Thoby soon passed to the Berners family,
who also acquired land at Fryerning. As a royal
auditor Sir William Berners was exceptionally
well placed to make such acquisitions. In 1541
Henry VIII granted the manor of South Weald to
Sir Brian Tuke, who rebuilt Weald Hall. South
Weald rapidly passed through several hands,
being inherited first by Tuke's son, Charles, then
his brother, George, before being sold to Sir

30. A Greene memorial in Navestock church, this one to a successful merchant of Navestock.

31. Another Greene memorial, this to a successful lawyer of Navestock.

Richard Rich in 1547 and sold on by him to Sir Anthony Browne. The manor of Abbess Warley passed to the Gonson family and remained in their hands until 1600. The manor of Bois Hall at Navestock came into the hands of the Greene family whose descendants became eminent lawyers, one becoming Recorder of London.

FOUNDING FATHER

Sir William Petre (?1505-72), founder of the oldest resident noble family in Essex, was by birth a Devon man. Educated at Exeter College, Oxford, he was elected a Fellow of All Souls in 1523 and proceeded to steep himself in civil and canon law. Serving as tutor to the future Viscount Rochford brought Petre the powerful patronage of the Boleyn family. Next attracting the notice of Thomas Cromwell, he proved a vigorous instrument in the suppression of the monasteries, extirpating the Gilbertines, the only purely English order, almost single-handed. The Petre as-

sociation with Ingatestone began in 1538 when he bought the manor of Gynge Abbess or Gynge at Petram (at the stone) formerly belonging to Barking Abbey. He pulled down Abbess Hall, replacing it with Ingatestone Hall *c.*1540 and renaming the manor Ging Petre alias Ingatestone. Petre survived Cromwell's disgrace and in 1543 was knighted and appointed secretary of state. In 1544 he was entrusted with assisting Queen Catherine as regent during the king's absence at war in France and in 1545 was sent as ambassador to the Holy Roman Emperor. Sworn of the privy council that same year, Petre rose still higher under Edward VI, serving him in matters diplomatic, ecclesiastical and financial and being entrusted to draw up the draft of the king's own will. Despite the fact that Petre had been among the commissioners appointed to tell the then Princess Mary that she was banned from holding Mass in her own household, Petre swiftly ingratiated himself and was invested with the Garter within months. Petre reciprocated by raising 142

32. Sir William Petre in 1567; artist unknown. Ten years into retirement he was still depicted with a wand and badge of office.

33. The gatehouse of Ingatestone Hall.

footmen from his Essex estates to oppose Wyatt's doomed rebellion against the queen in 1554 and then zealously hunting down Wyatt's accomplices. He further bolstered his standing with the queen by supporting her projected marriage with Philip II of Spain. Assiduous in his attendance at his sovereign's council, he acquiesced in the restoration of Catholicism – despite his own role in the Dissolution – and even used his by now formidable diplomatic expertise to extract from Pope Paul IV a bull confirming him in possession of the former monastic lands he had acquired. Ultimately his holdings were to amount to some 45,000 acres in nine counties, almost half in Essex. These included no less than five deer parks, an ultimate status symbol.

Declining health appears to have caused Petre to resign his post as secretary in 1557, though his illness may have been partly diplomatic, a tactful dissociation from the Queen's policy of burning Protestants. He continued to serve her successor intermittently. In 1564, for example, he took into custody at Ingatestone Hall Lady Catherine Seymour, Countess of Hertford (?1538-68), sister of the ill-fated Lady Jane Grey. Elizabeth herself

had visited Ingatestone Hall from the 19th to the 21st July 1561. This honour set the host back £136. After 1566 Petre lived in retirement at Ingatestone almost entirely, devoting much time to charitable projects, most notably the virtual re-foundation of his old Oxford college. A keen bibliophile and patron of Elizabeth's learned tutor Roger Ascham, Petre also endowed scholarships at All Souls and built almshouses in Ingatestone.

The local inhabitants may have found Sir William's retirement a mixed blessing as he proved to be a rare and rigorous upholder of the laws against such unlawful Sabbath recreations as cards, shove ha'penny (then known as slide groat), bowling and dice. In 1564-5 no less than fourteen men were presented for dice and bowls. After his death in 1572 there was only one further presentment locally for such offences before 1600. In 1568 he had even had three men reported for wearing apparel beyond their social status, an example, unique in the county, of an attempt to enforce sumptuary laws almost universally ignored.

Petre's will reveals the extent of his wealth, his interests and his obligations. A dozen silver

34. An interior of Ingatestone Hall showing family portraits.

spoons, a dozen silver trenchers and twenty further specified items of silver or gilt were specifically bequeathed to his widow, plus ten horses, all the livestock at Ingatestone, Writtle and East Horndon, ten featherbeds, half the household linen and the use of his London home in Aldersgate Street, rent-free for life. A gold ring with a diamond "given me by the Queen of good memory, Queen Mary" he designated to his daughter-in-law. Everything else went to Petre's son, John, except for nominal sums or items of silver to each of his four married daughters. He not only left forty pounds to the poor of Ingatestone and eight other nearby parishes but another thirty to parishes in Devon, Somerset, Kent and London, plus twenty "to the poorest prisoners in the prisons of London and Southwark", another twenty to the poor inmates of the hospitals of the same and an annuity of eighteen pounds for the Ingatestone almshouses, with "a black gown of coarse cloth" for each of their twenty inhabitants. In addition Petre left cash for five years' firewood for the local poor, for marriage portions for 'eight poor maids' and ten pounds to the restoration of the church. Five male

servants were left specified sums, four were left leases on farms, three more and the female housekeeper of Ingatestone Hall an annuity, all others a whole year's wages. There were also specific bequests to the executors and overseers of the will, twenty pounds to Lord Burleigh, forty pounds to Petre's alma mater, Exeter College, Oxford and the same sum to the rector of Ingatestone for serving Petre as his personal chaplain.

Petre's formidable daughter, Dorothy (1534-1618), married the immensely wealthy but reclusive Somerset landowner Nicholas Wadham and, as his executrix, became *de facto* founder of Wadham College, Oxford.

The year after his father's death Sir William Petre's only surviving son, John (1549-1613) bought West Horndon Hall, dating from 1414, and spent twenty years rebuilding it to become the family's principal seat, Thorndon Hall. John Petre was knighted in 1576, a singular mark of royal regard, the Queen being notoriously niggardly with knighthoods. Having served as Lord Lieutenant of Essex from 1575 until 1603, he was then created first Baron Petre of Writtle.

35. Old Thorndon Hall in 1669.

36. A seventeenth-century map showing the church and the symmetrically planted gardens and orchards around the manor house of West Horndon.

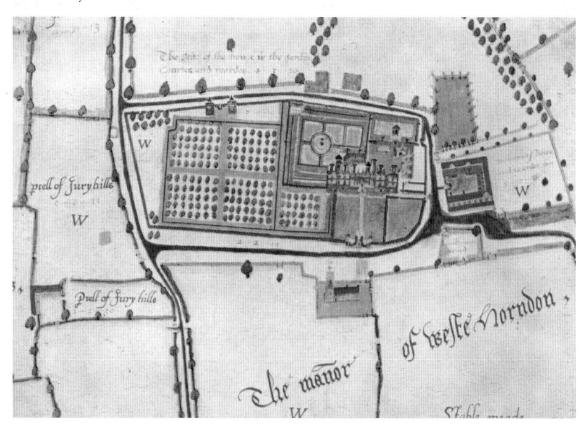

CHILDLESS FOUNDER

The career of Sir Anthony Browne (?1510-67) in many ways conformed to the pattern set by William Petre but to rather less effect. An Essex man by birth and the son of a knight to boot, Browne also went to Oxford but left without a degree, though this was not unusual. One went to Oxford for contacts rather than learning, which was to be found in London. Middle Temple inducted him into the law and in 1545 he served as MP for Lostwithiel in Cornwall. In 1553 Browne bought Weald Hall and the Brentwood manors of Calcot and Costed, once in the possession of Thomas Cromwell, from Anne of Cleves, Henry VIII's discarded fourth wife. In the same year he served as MP for Preston and in the following year represented Maldon. Under Mary he joined forces with Lord Rich, whose perjury had sent Sir Thomas More to the block, to eliminate Protestantism in Essex. In 1555 Browne was instrumental in securing the burning of one Watts at Chelmsford and teenage William Hunter at Brentwood *(see p42)*. In 1556 he was congratulated by the privy council for his successful pursuit of George 'Trudge over the world' Eagles, a tailor and itinerant preacher, whom Browne adjudged traitor as well as heretic, thus condemning him

to be hanged, drawn and quartered. In 1558 Browne's zeal was rewarded by appointment as Chief Justice of Common Pleas. His tenure was, however, but brief, Elizabeth demoting him to the rank of puisne judge. She did, however, knight him in 1566. Browne died the following year, without issue, his most lasting legacy being the grammar school he had founded in 1557 and to which he made over his manor of Chigwell Grange. The almshouses he had built in Wigley Bush Lane in 1563 were rebuilt in the eighteenth century and again in the nineteenth century.

Browne's will reflects both his legal career and his Catholicism. It specifically requested that he be buried with Catholic rites and left bequests for "the new founded houses at Grey Friars and Bridewell". It also specified a bequest to Serjeants Inn, 'whereof I am', the return of ancient law books to his Mordaunt relatives and to the family of his old teacher and two pounds for the relief of inmates of four London prisons. Legacies for local benefit included cash for the poor and towards highway repairs and the marriage costs of his labourers' offspring. Modest personal bequests were made to his sister's two lame children and to such Essex eminenti as Sir William Petre, Lord Rich and members of the Waldegrave,

37. A Prospect of Weald Hall, by William van der Hagen.

38. Queen Mary's Chapel gained its name from its association with Catholic worship rather than with the monarch herself.

Tyrrell, Mordaunt, Huddlestone and White families. The bulk of Browne's estate passed to his great-nephew, Wistan Browne, who died in 1581. Wistan's high-handed behaviour *(see p.46)* made him unpopular locally, a fact implicitly acknowledged in his will by the proviso that "at the day of my funerals dole be given to the poor people, viz. 6d apiece to so many of them as will hold up their hands to take it."

A MUSICAL MARGINAL

Against the rapid social mobility of Tudor England must be set the treacherous cross-currents created by shifts in religious and political allegiance which could exalt or destroy both indi-

viduals and whole families, depending on how they could reconcile conscience and conformity. Composer William Byrd (1540-1623), pioneer of the English madrigal, clung to the old faith but managed to live at Stondon Place, Stondon Massey for nearly thirty years. As a courtier he might be thought to have ranked with or even above gentry status, but he seems to have welcomed gentry protection. The details of Byrd's early life are obscure, save that he was "bred up to musick under Thomas Tallis", "the father of English church music". Organist at Lincoln in his twenties, Byrd was appointed organist to the Chapel Royal in 1569, sharing the post with Tallis. They also shared a highly lucrative twenty-one year monopoly on the production of printed music and musical manuscript paper. Despite his high-profile position at the heart of the Elizabethan establishment Byrd remained a firm Catholic. As a recusant he deemed it prudent, however, to live at some distance from the capital, initially at Harlington in Middlesex. Byrd appears to have acquired a lease of Stondon Place around 1593, when its owner, William Shelley, ironically a Catholic, was convicted of high treason. Byrd's possession was later contested by Shelley's widow until her death in 1609, when Byrd finally bought Stondon Place in the names of John and Thomas Petre, an arrangement which led to further litigation after his death. Byrd's extraordinary musical talent appears to have protected him from the more rigorous consequences of his attachment to a proscribed faith. He also doubtless benefited from the protection of the powerful Petre family, with whom he was on terms of close friendship. Excommunicated in 1598, Byrd still participated in James I's coronation. From 1605 to 1612 he and his family were regularly recorded by the archdiaconal court of Essex as being "papisticall recusants", with Mrs Byrd apparently zealously intent on making converts of her neighbours. Byrd's contemporary standing can be judged from the praise lavished on him in a handbook for arrivistes *The Compleat Gentleman* (1622): "In Motets and Musicke of pietie and devotion, as well for the honour of our Nation, as the merit of the Man, I preferre above all other ... Mr. William Byrd, whom in that kind I know not whether any may equall, I am sure, none excell, even by the judgment of France and Italy ...". Posterity has done little to amend this verdict. Byrd was a prolific and versatile composer, producing three Masses, songs for the stage and many works for the virginals, as well as pioneering the verse anthem with its alternation of solo and choral passages.

Byrd had six children. Thomas, son of Byrd's eldest son Christopher, was living at Stondon in 1631-2. The house was rebuilt in 1700, burned down in 1877 and rebuilt once more on the old foundations. It is assumed that Byrd was buried in the village churchyard though no gravesite is known.

RICH ENOUGH

Sir Nathaniel Rich (?1585-1636) was probably the eldest son of Richard Rich, bastard son of Richard, first baron Rich, betrayer of St Thomas More and founder of Felsted school. The other side of

39. William Byrd. The Italian caption testifies to his international reputation.

Sir Nathaniel's family had a City background, his mother being the daughter of John Machell, sometime sheriff of London. Trained as a lawyer and admitted to Gray's Inn in 1610, Rich chose to pursue commerce via politics. Assiduous politicking enabled him to ride out the discontinuities created by a sequence of short-lived parliaments which might have scuppered the public career of a less determined man. In 1614 he sat as Member for Totnes in distant Devon. In 1617 he managed to get himself knighted, an honour admittedly in plentiful supply at the Stuart court – for a price. By 1621 he was representing East Retford in Nottinghamshire and the following year served as a member of a royal commission in Ireland. In 1624-5 he represented the port of Harwich, then briefly Newport – Isle of Wight, not Essex – then Harwich again from 1626 to 1629. Rich's connections with commerce began in 1616 with an interest in the Bermudas Company, to which in 1619 he added shares in the by then flourishing Virginia Company, which had survived the early catastrophes of its Jamestown settlement and found salvation – economic, rather than spiritual – in tobacco. Of the latter Company Rich was to become a prominent member. When the Virginia Company split into two contending factions in 1623 Rich, not suprisingly, sided with his kinsman, Robert Rich, second earl of Warwick.

In 1629 Rich and Warwick headed a consortium to fund a voyage of exploration to Providence Island, off Mexico and the following year received a patent confirming them as the company of adventurers for the plantation of Providence and Henrietta, the latter diplomatically named for the new French queen. Rich became the leading spirit in the effort to bring this venture to realisation, handling its legal affairs and proving his good faith by being the first to respond to further cash calls. Named deputy governor of the company in 1635, he enjoyed his office for only a year before dying. Sir Nathaniel Rich was buried, at his express wish, at Stondon, where he was lord of the manor. His will contained several bequests to the Rich family and to schools in the Bermudas. Stondon passed to a nephew, also Nathaniel, possibly the Cromwellian colonel who, after a colourful career in war and politics, died in 1701.

THE WRIGHT STUFF

The Wright family acquired Kelvedon Hall in 1538 and stayed in possession for the next four centuries. John Wright of Kelvedon Hall died in 1551. His second son, Robert (died 1587), became lord of the manor of Great and Little Ropers, occupying the Moat House at Brook Street. Members of the family were among the early migrants to New England during the 'Great Migration' of the 1630s. One of John Wright's direct descendants, Thomas, was clerk to the General Court of Wethersfield, Connecticut in 1643. The Wright brothers, pioneers of powered flight, traced their ancestry to the same family.

LESS LORDLY

F G Emmison's painstaking analysis of Essex gentry wills provides much material illustrative of the lifestyles, concerns and obligations of the interlocking lives of local Tudor notabilities below the exalted rank of the Petres. Some were just, others very far, below.

Robert Pascall (died 1570) of Mountnessing was styled as a yeoman but, apart from his farm there, known as Bacons, also held lands in Little Burstead, Buttsbury, Stock, Great Baddow, Sandon, Inworth and Tolleshunt D'Arcy. The two last were each sizeable operations in their own right, the former having twenty cows, a bull and twenty ewes, the latter a bull, forty-six cows, a hundred and twenty ewes and three colts. Thomas Porter (died 1577) another Mountnessing yeoman owned two houses and held parcels of land in Stondon Massey, Blackmore, Doddinghurst, Navestock and Galleywood Common. These were bequeathed to his wife and two sons but he was also sufficiently wealthy to leave £120 to be divided among his three daughters.

John Drywood, gentleman (died 1579), owned properties outright in Dunton, Little Burstead, and Childerditch, as well as the White Hart in Brentwood; but he was also a tenant of both Sir Henry Tyrrell and Sir John Petre. After making the usual careful arrangements for the maintenance of his widow during her lifetime, Drywood left the bulk of his property to his eldest son John, bidding him maintain his younger brother, Thomas, at school and "one of the universities". Bequests were left to Drywood's mother-in-law, Lady Petre, the parson of Dunton, eight other named persons, all his godchildren and maidservants and to the poor in no less than eighteen parishes and 'the town of Brentwood'. A further fifty pounds was left for mourning clothes for ten of his tenants who would act as his pall-bearers.

John Peers of Mountnessing, (died 1584), appears to have retired there fairly recently from the City because he left more for the poor of Bread Street ward than for local indigents, as well as an equal sum for a feast in his memory for the wardens of the Fishmongers' Company. The detailed inventory of his goods reveals a musical household, possessing a pair of virginals and six viols. It also shows that his house, 'Arnoldes', had a 'great parlour', a hall, little parlour, 'great chamber', counting house, five further upstairs chambers, including one for the maids, plus a kitchen, a pantry and a long gallery, which sounds impressive but apparently contained only bedsteads, although a portrait did hang in the great parlour. Outside stood a 'great millhouse', brewhouse and dairyhouse. Although four gold rings were left to Peers' daughter and two sons-in-law, there is no mention at all of any item of plate, let alone books or armour, so the Peers establishment must be judged a rather homely one.

George White of Hutton Hall, (died 1584), also held the manors of Rivenhall, Thundersley Hall and Runwell Hall and part of Rawreth. He also had a "blue waggon or coach", an unusual luxury item and still quite a novelty for a country gentleman. The close relationships among local gentry are revealed in his concern to leave a gold ring each to "Sir Edmund Huddlestone and Mr. Thomas Tyrrell, my good friends" and "my especial and good friend Sir John Peter ... one of my best geldings which I would were worth £1,000 to him."

John Barkley, (died 1587), was another retiree from the capital, having been serjeant of the Queen's Cellar. He had managed to accumulate properties in Collier Row, Chigwell and Enfield but his own Shenfield home was held on a lease and he made no bequests apart from those to his four children, two servants and two executors.

The will of John Cliff of Ingatestone, (died 1589), attests the power of the Petres in opening with the bequest of gold rings to Sir John and his wife with the request to "continue their goodwill towards my poor children". Cliff had three married daughters and one son, a lawyer in Middle Temple, who inherited his father's house, Bedells, and seven other properties in Ingatestone, amounting to over 120 acres, as well as land in eight other parishes. Cliff also left the usual bequest for the local poor but "in no wise to give any to vagabonds". This was evidently a matter on which he held strong views because he specified that six pounds should also be given "towards the maintaining of the house of correction for vagabonds erected at Coggeshall." Cliff directed that he "not be buried with any solemnity but only in honest and sober sort" but he did countenance the erection of a monument with his name and the names of his two wives.

The will of John Bentley (died 1602), 'servant to Sir John Peter' reveals much about the cultured lifestyle of the Petre household. Bentley's son George was to receive not only "my great ring of gold which I daily wear" but also "all my sets of song books and songs in rolls and my books for the virginals ... all ... my dictionaries in Greek or Latin or other languages ... all my books pertaining to divinity ... my statute books and law books, one pair of virginals, my maps and arms, one silver bowl, two silver spoons, my best gown and my best cloak." Bentley left to his employer "my new bible in Latin in quarto of Venice print" and to Lady Petre "a very fruitful and pleasant book called the Instruction of a Christian Woman" and twenty shillings in gold – which compares rather favourably with the one silver spoon and deal chest he left to his eldest daughter.

John Colvyle of Brentwood, who died in 1602, is described as a gentleman. His bequests to his wife included a gold chain and unspecified quantities of cash, jewels, plate, corn and cattle. These may not have amounted to a great sum because his specific cash bequests were fairly modest – ten pounds a year for life for his wife, from the profits of the Swan Inn in Brentwood, two pounds likewise for his father, twenty pounds outright to each of two daughters and a pound each to his brother and three sisters and the poor of Brentwood and Hundon in Suffolk. Colvyle's "lands in Ingrave" – unspecified in type or amount – he left to his only son.

Compared to Colvyle, Henry Rolf of Kelvedon Hatch, whose will was proved in 1603, seems more like a magnate than a mere gentleman. He was able to bequeath his eldest daughter, Mary, five hundred pounds, plus the leases on his own dwelling house in St Lawrence Lane in the City of London and grazing lands in Mucking, Corringham and Horndon-on-the-Hill. She also received "a double gilt bowl of silver", three horses, twelve cows and a bull, twenty ewes and a quantity of bedding. His married daughter Anne received his freehold lands in Shenfield and the lease of "houses new built by me" in Grub Street, on the northern fringe of the City, on the condition of distributing thirteen penny loaves a week among the poor of St Giles-without-Cripplegate. Anne also received £200 not yet paid from her promised dowry of £500 as well as twenty ewes, six cows and a bedstead. But all Anne's benefits were conditional on her father-in-law making over to her and her husband lands to the annual value of £80. A third daughter, Elizabeth, also married, likewise received £500 and "my messuage called Brizes, with the lands belonging in Kelvedon, Navestock and Doddinghurst " and the lease of the farm called Jennynges. Presumably to avoid unseemly bickering Rolf ordered that his plate, jewels, gold and linen should be divided by his executors into three portions of equal value and that his three daughters should pull lots out of a hat to decide who got which.

Rolf's brother and two brothers-in-law owed him over £900 between them. This he ordered to be distributed among their families. He also left his brother, a sister, sister-in-law, cousin and cousin's wife and four other persons money for a gold ring to be worn in memory of him. One of the brothers-in-law also got Rolf's 'best livery gown'. His apparently impoverished cousin, Robert received £50 plus £20 for his daughter at marriage or 21 and £5 to his son, plus "such apparel of my own or my wife's as my executor shall think meet to him and Anne his wife." Rolf's bequests to his two god-children, manservant and two maidservants of £1 each seem niggardly beside such generosity. Five pounds was left to the poor of his birthplace, Sperle, in Norfolk, two to the poor of Kelvedon "where I dwell", a pound each to Stondon, Blackmore, South Weald, Navestock and Doddinghurst and fifteen shillings each to the two Ongars. The poor of these parishes were also to receive between them a bullock and ten bushels of wheat and six barrels of beer – excepting any who misbehaved at his funeral.

The Daily Round

THE WORLD OF WORK

In 1594 the topographer John Norden described Essex as the English Goshen, "most fatt, frutefull and full of profitable things, exceeding ... any other shire, the fattest of the Land, comparable to Palestina, that flowed with milk and honey". Its agricultural output had the most varied range of output of any county. Hops, which transformed traditionally flat ale into beer with a bite, are known to have been growing at Ingatestone Hall as early as 1548, less than twenty years since they had been introduced to England from Germany. Improvements in brewing naturally encouraged the production of barley on a substantial scale. In the 1580s Norden's predecessor, William Camden, had remarked on the "cheeses of extraordinary bigness", made from ewes' milk in the marshy pasture areas of south-east Essex. Many of these were sold for ships' stores. Cattle fattening was another marshland speciality. Stock driven long distances for sale in the capital became stringy en route and needed to be rested and restored before being offered to the buyer.

Brentwood's fair, especially noted for cattle, was one of the half dozen most important in the county, the others being at Newport, Epping, Harlow and Romford – i.e. on the major roads leading to London. The lesser ones were at Coggeshall, Little Dunmow, Thaxted and Chelmsford.

Lying as it did in a fertile farming area, Brentwood's commerce was therefore dominated by grocers, cheesemen, butchers and bakers, catering to the needs of both local residents not employed in agriculture, to the insatiable demands of England's greatest city and to the many travellers passing through on their way to or from the capital. Other retailers included mercers, dealing in the finer types of cloth, and fellmongers, who dealt in hides, especially sheepskins. Fellmongers and tanners dealt in their turn with local workers in leather, such as cobblers and saddlers, who worked in the heavier grades, and glovers and cordwainers, who crafted the finer ones. Tudor Brentwood, although not a significant textile centre like Braintree, Halstead or Coggeshall, did have weavers, as well as tailors and specialist collarmakers. Some retailers operated on a more than local scale. William Cocke, a Brentwood linendraper, also had a market stall in Chelmsford. When a thief broke into Richard

40. A shepherd and neat-herd, 1579. It contrasts ragged herdsmen with contented livestock.

41. Ploughing in 1523. Woodcut from Fitzherbert's Boke of Husbondrye.

Hesseldyne's shop in Ingatestone in 1590 he carried away sixteen dozen bone-laces, two pounds of pepper, four pounds of ginger, a pound of cinnamon, twenty thousand pins and a thousand needles – striking evidence of luxurious tastes in the locality.

Apart from the sort of gentry whose custom Hesseldyne doubtless valued, there were also some members of the emergent professional classes in the locality, such as teachers and scriveners, who drafted wills, bonds, leases and other legal documents. Whether John Fyssher, barber-surgeon of Brentwood, might be called a professional is open to doubt. In 1583 he was acquitted of murder, having, at West Ham, thrown a bricklayer to the ground twice so violently that he died later the same day, the death being attributed to another assailant, unknown. Four years later the same Fyssher had "taken upon himself to cure a broken leg" caused by a beer barrel falling off a cart. He "warranted the right placing of the bones and the perfect health of the same

leg." He took his fee, but the patient died.

The will of John Ammat, proved in 1592, shows that by that date even a small place like West Horndon could have a surgeon in residence. It is quite likely, of course, that he had retired there after quitting a practice located somewhere much bigger. Ammat's relatively modest standing is indicated by the fact that although he bequeathed to friends such costly items as a rapier, a distilling apparatus and "my jewel set in gold", he left no real estate and made no cash bequest greater than ten pounds. His surgical instruments and books were left to his major beneficiary, his brother Thomas.

The volume of freight passing through Brentwood kept blacksmiths, coopers and wheelwrights in employment, while its gradual expansion and the upgrading of properties occasioned by 'the Great Rebuilding' of 1540-1640 gave work to the bricklayer, sawyer, plumber, glazier and thatcher. Thomas Danwood alias Beane had two anvils and specialised in horse-shoeing. John Darbye a Brentwood blacksmith who died in 1560 is known to have had a sideline in making nails. Brick-making was carried on at East Horndon and tile-making at Ingatestone.

The necessarily uncertain nature of an agrarian economy, dependent on climate and seasons, was partly offset by the opportunities of expanding commerce. Multiple occupations were not uncommon. One Ingrave bachelor made tiles in summer but worked as a tailor in winter. The law, however, set limits on versatility. In 1572 a petition was presented to the County Bench by five mercers of Brentwood to complain that five tailors, a smith, a labourer and a widow of neighbouring rural parishes "unlawfully use the occupations of mercers, haberdashers and grocers" without having served an apprenticeship. Their grievance was supported by six Chelmsford men.

Naturally the law required not only the standards of quality supposedly guaranteed by the service of formal apprenticeship but also an orderly and honest conduct of business. In 1590 Michael Hardman of Margaretting was prosecuted for brawling in the churchyard of Ingatestone on the day of its fair. In the same year Brentwood was reported for not having properly authenticated standard measures, a charge repeated the following year, there being "no market bushel nor other sealed measures, greatly to the hindrance of the poor", who, presumably were most apt to be cheated. Nor was commercial malfeasance necessarily a petty matter of short-weight or adulteration. In 1599 Judith Townsend, a widow and her accomplices, Daniel Wylson and Richard Barle, were indicted for the crime of engrossing (buying up to hoard) 20,000lbs of butter worth £300 at Brentwood.

The management of the rural environment on which all ultimately depended was also closely regulated. Offences against good order and practice documented in the records of the manor court of Ingatestone include admonitions and fines for unscoured ditches and unlopped roadside trees, for hedge breaking and allowing stock – especially diseased animals – to stray. Wood-stealers were warned that they would be whipped half-naked until they "bleed well". Another offence was felling wood without leaving staddles, young trees to provide re-growth. In 1567 a Shenfield court fined a Brentwood man for digging two cartloads of clay without licence. At Navestock in 1603 John Howe was fined for unauthorised cutting of gorse.

Failure to maintain the infrastructure deemed essential for community life was also subject to the wrath of the justices. In the 1560s the archery butts in Childerditch were found to be out of repair and a ten shilling fine threatened for failing to make them good again. This was a common enough offence at the time and the likelihood is that nothing was actually done about either the butts or the fine. The bridge at 'Gynge Mountneye' (Mountnessing) was similarly reported as ruinous. Bridge maintenance was often contentious, the structures visibly deteriorating as various interested parties attempted to shrug off responsibility for repair onto each other.

HEARTH AND HOME

In his *Description of England* William Harrison (1577) noted at length and with some wonder the changes in domestic comfort that he had seen in his own lifetime. Men whose fathers had slept on straw, with a bag of grain for a pillow, now slept in linen, with hangings to keep out the cold. They ate off pewter platters, instead of wooden trenchers, sitting on chairs, rather than benches or stools, at joiner-made tables, rather than at boards balanced on trestles. Their houses now boasted such luxuries as fireplaces with chimneys, floors of wood, rather than of trodden earth, and windows of glass, rather than draughty shutters. How far does the Brentwood area bear out Harrison's claim for what might be called a 'comfort revolution'?

A selection of wills proved before the Bishop of London's Commissary Court in the period 1587-99 provides varied evidence of the life styles

42. *The simple Doddinghurst cottage, built from local materials, represented typical housing for the moderately prosperous.*

of those of 'the meaner sort' who stood below the gentry but still had something to bequeath, even if, as in the case of Thomas Petchie, a Blackmore wheelwright and joiner, the sole movable items held to be of value consisted of the tools of his trade or in the case of Thomas Robjont, a Blackmore yeoman, a black mare. What was deemed movable has changed since then. Thomas Storgyn of Ingatestone felt obliged to state specifically that " all the glass windows to remain in the house."

Beds and bedding certainly figure prominently as prized possessions, as do garments and better-made items of furniture. Richard Brighte, a farmer of Great Warley, distributed no less than six different sorts of chest to various beneficiaries but left a dripping pan and spit to his only son. William Lacye, another Great Warley man, distributed sheep, a cow, a mare, a gelding and a leather doublet and hose. A Blackmore butcher, appropriately named John Hogge, divided his land equally between his three daughters but additionally left to the eldest a 'hutch' (chest or coffer) and its unspecified contents, along with what were evidently his late spouse's treasures "the best gown, best petticoat, a kirtle, a great chest which was my wife's" plus "a joined standing bedstead and two featherbeds ... and the cupboard in the parlour." Butchers could be quite well off. William Wolston of Great Warley left his wife a house and land at Shenfield and his daughters twenty pounds each. Edward Finch, a Fryerning butcher left a house and barn with fifteen acres, two other plots of seven acres and a separate garden plot.

Attitudes towards spouses and offspring are frequently revealed in the careful wording of bequests. It was normal to designate not only an executor to carry out the provisions of a will but also overseers, often including the local clergyman, to ensure that this had been properly done. Alice Pawmer of Fryerning performed a fine balancing act with her three daughters, willing the first "my best petticoat, best kirtle, my bed and bedstead", while the second got "my best gown, second kettle and my cupboard", leaving the third to be content with "my furred gown, worst kirtle and worst petticoat." Robert Chamberlayne, an Ingatestone labourer, left the use of his goods to his widow for the remainder of her life but specified that "if she needeth to sell anything for her maintenance it shall be done with the advice of my overseer." John Gynkyns,

a smith of Ingatestone, required that all his goods be sold and the proceeds invested, to be distributed equally among his five children as they came of age at twenty-one. William Wall of Ingatestone decreed that if any of his children troubled his widow about their legacy they should lose it.

The relative worth of different types of possession is indicated where a will is accompanied by an appraisal. The bedding belonging to Anne Browne of Ingatestone – a featherbed, two flockbeds and a bedstead – at 23s 4d was worth more than all her other furniture (a cupboard, square table, three chests and three chairs = twelve shillings) and her household linen (ten shillings) added together. Her one item of livestock, a heifer valued at 33s 4d, was deemed far more valuable than all her other possessions, consisting of iron work (2s 6d), pewter (2s) and brassware and clothing each valued at the conventional sum of half a mark (6s 8d). Interestingly her entire estate was quite dwarfed in value by the debts owed to her, more than seventeen pounds.

ARMADA!

Brentwood's strategic location, straddling the road to Harwich but within easy reach of the Thames, has made it a periodic place of assembly for military forces at times of threat or civil disorder. In 1588, when the country was placed in the highest state of readiness to counter an anticipated invasion by the mighty Spanish Armada, the Queen's favourite, Robert Dudley, Earl of Leicester, appointed Brentwood as a rendezvous point for contingents from eight eastern and midland counties. The Spanish fleet was first sighted on 19 July and on the 23rd the counties were ordered to send their cavalry to arrive at Brentwood by the 27th. Nine hundred horsemen assembled, with an arsenal of 120 barrels of gunpowder, before proceeding to the great armed camp at Tilbury where Elizabeth I reviewed the host gathered there to oppose the expected landing. Although "God blew and they were scattered" the fear of invasion remained. There were two more substantial assemblies in 1597 and 1599, bringing contingents from as far away as Norfolk and Suffolk. An emergency reserve of a dozen barrels of gunpowder was kept in a private house and Brentwood remained the mustering place for the hundreds of Chafford, Barstable, Beacontree, Harlow and Ongar.

Conscience and Controversy

EXAMPLE AND TERROR

Henry VIII may have repudiated the authority of the Pope, despoiled the monasteries and put an English Bible in every parish church but, in terms of fundamental doctrine, he remained a traditional Catholic. Determined that his subjects should be equally orthodox he had Parliament pass the Statute of Six Articles, reaffirming the basic tenets of belief. In May 1546 Edmund Bonner, Bishop of London came to Brentwood to try several local residents indicted for denying the doctrine of transubstantiation, i.e. that during the Mass bread and wine were literally transformed into the body and blood of Christ. Five of the accused were found guilty. The King pardoned two but ordered that John Camper, Thomas Skygges and Joan Bette should be executed "at Colchester and two other places within the Countie most mete for thexample and terrour of others."

Nine years later another denial of the same doctrine produced the same outcome. William Hunter was a nineteen-year-old silk-weaver's apprentice who was dismissed by his London master on account of his passionate Protestantism which, during the Catholic reaction under Queen Mary, might well have imperilled both the master's business and family. Returning to his native Brentwood, Hunter became involved in a disputation with Thomas Wood, Vicar of South Weald and Chaplain of St Thomas's in Brentwood. Hunter's denial of the doctrine of transubstantiation led to an interview with the local magistrate 'Master Browne', who passed him on to Bishop Bonner. Bonner argued with Hunter at length until the latter's recalcitrance earned him two days in the stocks. Public humiliation failing to shift Hunter's attitude, Bonner sent him to prison. Over a period of nine months Bonner re-interviewed Hunter no less than five times. On the fifth occasion he not only offered him yet another opportunity to recant but is alleged further to have offered him the option of either a grant of forty pounds to set up in business for himself or even a position in the bishop's own household, if only he would return to the orthodox fold. Hunter refusing yet again, he was

43. *The Martyr's Tree – memorialised in Brentwood School's school song.*

confined in Newgate for a further month, then returned to Brentwood for execution.

Hunter is said to have been lodged at the Swan Inn prior to his immolation. Arriving on the Saturday immediately before the Feast of the Annunciation, he was held over until the following Tuesday rather than mar a major landmark in the Catholic sacerdotal calendar. Hunter received last visits from his parents and friends until finally he was burned at the stake "at the town's end, where the butts stood" in the presence of the townspeople, including magistrate Sir Anthony Browne. Tradition assigned the site of Hunter's martyrdom to a great elm tree whose dead trunk was replaced by an oak to mark the accession of George VI in 1936. Brentwood School's school song indirectly claims that Browne founded the school as an act of contrition for his part in the proceedings. Whatever his personal motivation his action cannot be interpreted as an act of gesture politics to ingratiate himself with the revived Protestant regime under Elizabeth I. Royal licence to found the school was granted by Mary in July 1558, four months before her death.

The persecution of Protestants under Mary was succeeded by the persecution of Catholics under

44. *Memorial to Protestant martyr, William Hunter at Brentwood erected in the mid-Victorian era, despite the fact that at the time there was a sizeable Roman Catholic population in the area.*

Elizabeth. John Payne, one time steward of Stondon Hall, converted to Catholicism, trained at the English College in Douai and after ordination in 1576 returned to England, becoming chaplain to the Dowager Lady Petre, but passing himself off as her household steward. Having been briefly detained and released in 1577, in 1581 he was taken into custody for allegedly plotting to assassinate the Queen and then racked in a vain effort to extort a confession. His accuser, George Elliot, a former member of the Petre household staff, may have been acting from a personal grudge and, according to the accused Payne, was a man of the worst character with a long criminal record as an embezzler, fraudster, rapist and suspected murderer. Elliot was rewarded for his 'evidence' with the huge sum of a £100. (Compare this with the £136 it cost Sir William Petre to entertain Elizabeth I and her entourage for three whole days.) Payne protested that "it was against the law of God and man that he should be condemned for one man's witness notoriously infamous." The judge blithely responded that had Payne been not guilty the jury would have found him so. Payne replied that "those

men of the jury were but poor, simple men, nothing at all understanding what treason is..." – to no avail. Payne suffered the agonising death of a traitor – hanged, drawn and quartered at Chelmsford the following year. He was finally canonised in 1970 as one of forty English Martyrs. Ingatestone's almshouses are dedicated to his memory.

Apart from the Petres other notable recusant families included the Waldegraves of Navestock, the Whites of Hutton and the Wrights of South Weald. In 1590 Mary, wife of John Wright of the Moat House, Brook Street, was arraigned as an obstinate recusant who kept "one Rodes scoolmaster that teacheth her children privately, the which children do not come to church neither."

PASTORAL FAILINGS

The Elizabethan determination to impose uniformity of worship was impeded by both ecclesiastical inadequacies and at least passive resistance in the locality.

The failings of the clergy were sometimes matters of duty. In 1565 it was reported that George Colborne, parson of Little Warley, had

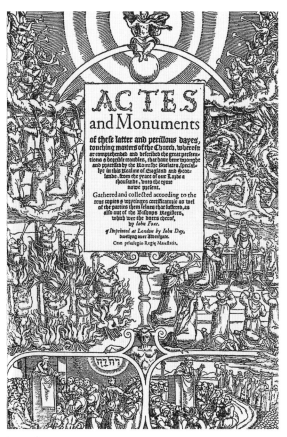

45. William Hunter's story is one of almost 300 recorded in John Foxe's Actes and Monuments – *after the Bible, the most widely owned book in Elizabethan England.*

46. A window at Ingatestone church. After the Reformation the gentry, depicting their heraldic motifs, replaced the Church as patrons of stained glass makers.

been absent for five years and William Newhouse of Shenfield for fifteen months. John Sherebourne of Great Warley was also reported as an absentee who had left his parish in the charge of "rude and unlearned persons" for months at a time. Newhouse was deprived of his living in 1567 but Colborne kept his – and in 1579 his servant Eleanor Jellson was accused of receiving a man not her husband into Colborne's house. In 1566 the rector of West Horndon was accused of "not having sermons, contrary to the Queen's Injunctions". At Buttsbury "the parson hath not examined the parents neither the godfather nor godmother of their belief in the time of baptism ... neither hath instructed the youth in the catechism." In 1584 the incumbent of Blackmore was censured because "two children died unchristened by his negligence, for that he would not christen them before Sunday following, and died in the meantime."

Sometimes priestly shortcomings were matters of personal morality. In 1564 the rector of East Horndon was condemned for luring other men's servants into gambling. His humiliation was "to stand in the mid place of the church with his surplice and a white rod in his hand, confessing that he hath done evil in alluring the youth to play at tables and to give 20d to the poor." In 1565 the rector of Fryerning was suspected of unchastity with a servant; she claimed a blood relationship and was exonerated. In 1588 his successor was denounced as "an alehouse haunter". In 1584 a Blackmore parishioner was arraigned for "calling the minister whoremaster knave". Two years later the minister, Edward Binder, was charged that "he pays honest women to commit adultery with him". He failed to prove his innocence and was obliged to do public penance and suspended.

CONTRARY CONGREGATIONS

Passive resistance towards the officially ordained setting and modes of worship took numerous forms. In 1564 the churchwardens of South Weald were ordered "forthwith to cause the superstitious images to be defaced." Kelvedon Hatch and Childerditch were judged tardy in setting up appropriate communion tables. In 1565 Little Warley and East Horndon were ordered to convert their chalices into communion cups. Fryerning said Sir William Petre would pay for theirs to be done. Ingatestone was ordered to acquire one. In 1568 the churchwardens of Shenfield were indicted for not having a copy of the approved book of homilies and a cover for the communion cup. In 1569, a full decade after action was ordered, there still remained a rood loft in Ingrave church and at West Horndon an actual rood. Later it was explained that pulling the entire rood-loft down at West Horndon might endanger the church itself. Both these survivals were probably attributable to the staunchly Catholic Lord Mordaunt (died 1570), a former privy councillor to Mary. In much the same way John Tyrrell, Catholic lord of the manor of Little Warley, refused to allow the pulling down of "a beam whereon was wont to stand a light before an image called Our Lady". In 1569 also three of Mordaunt's servants observed the traditional custom of ringing peals of bells for the souls of the departed on All Hallows' Eve, contrary to the new Anglican decree. (The sexton of Kelvedon Hatch had been similarly indicted in 1563 and two men likewise at Moutnessing in 1564.)

Occasionally there were instances of blatant neglect. In 1561 Mountnessing steeple was recorded as ruined and in 1580 its chancel. In 1571 the chancel windows at Little Warley were badly broken "whereby owlets cometh in and thereby with dung bewrayed." In 1589 the Fryerning churchwardens were accused of pulling down the church porch and selling it off. They excused themselves on the grounds that it had not been much used, was very small and had, in any case, all been done with the consent of the whole parish. They were ordered to replace it with a new one.

And then there was the normal spectrum of human frailty to excuse non-attendance at church. In 1562 at Midlent Stondon and Kelvedon had an inter-village football match, followed by "play at the cards all night" and, for some, bowls the morning after as well. In the same decade two tapsters and two bricklayers of Shenfield, with unnamed others, played football on Passion Sunday. Not only was such a diversion at such a time impious it was also disapproved as a frequent cause of violence.

In 1564 Michael Lylle of Fryerning sought exemption for absence from church by pleading that "I am Sir William Petre's man and cannot come and I am a smith". He was ordered to do penance in church and give fourpence to the poor. In the same year another offender was ordered to do his penance in Brentwood market-place. In 1565 it was reported that large numbers at South Weald and Great Warley had failed to take communion even a minimum three times in the year and Shenfield reported three parishioners who, when they should have been at a church service, either "kept ill rule" or "danceth the morris". In 1587 John Petchie and his wife of Fryerning were reported for "keeping their child unchristened three weeks". Four South Weald men pleaded in 1590 that "upon necessity they are sometimes invited to their friends, as to a bride-ale, and sometimes to dinner, and sometimes are visited with sickness". In 1591 William Cock of Little Warley was successfully discharged for non-attendance at church on the grounds that "sometime he went to West Horndon to service and to Sir John Petre's to dinner, for he works there commonly".

Henry Gray of South Weald was rebuked for practising dancing during sermon time and for 'dancing the morris home' with the bridegroom after a wedding in 1604, making "rather a May game of marriage than a holy institution of God."

What is striking about this frequently laggardly behaviour is that Essex was supposed to be a hotbed of Puritan fervour, while recusancy was characteristic of regions far from the metropolis, like Lancashire – apparently not.

Outright sedition, however, was treated with swift severity, even if it might seem to have been little more than meretricious gossip. In 1560 Anne Dowe of Brentwood was imprisoned for saying that the Queen was pregnant by court favourite Robert Dudley. In 1576 Mary Cleere of Ingatestone was found guilty of saying the Queen was "baseborn and not born to the Crown but that another lady was the right inheritor", for which she was sentenced to the hideous death of being drawn and burned. In 1587 Edward Tabor, a Fryerning innkeeper, was charged with uttering seditious words against the Queen. He was dismissed from his office as constable and imprisoned for some months in Colchester castle but eventually discharged without further action.

PROTESTANT PROTESTS

If Anglican uniformity met with sloth and occasional sedition from the religious right, as it were, it also encountered resistance from the left as well. Four years after William Hunter's demise the court roll of Costed manor records that John Tyler and two others cut down a cross then standing in Brentwood's High Street. Bailiff Thomas Mall took charge of the cross pending discussion with Sir Anthony Browne as lord of the manor and local magistrate but what exactly transpired remains unknown. The fact that the court rolls contain no further reference to the incident might be taken as negative evidence that this minor act of iconoclasm had been implicitly condoned, given that the accession of Elizabeth had abruptly ended the abortive Catholic counter-Reformation.

In 1574 Thomas Reddriche, puritan vicar of Childerditch, was presented at Quarter Sessions for refusing to wear a surplice. A decade later, as vicar of Hutton, his preaching was attracting recalcitrant souls from Doddinghurst and he was accused of preaching at a conventicle (banned puritan meeting), which he denied, claiming that he dined at a certain house on a date he could not remember, with people whose names he could not remember and that he had only answered questions put to him. The curate of Doddinghurst was accused of not wearing a surplice in 1583. In 1606 Reddriche's successor at Childerditch, Arthur Grove, was indicted for the same offence and for refusing to make the sign of the cross when performing baptisms. Ralph Hawkdon of Fryerning was indicted in 1587 on precisely the same charges and was subsequently dismissed.

Deviations from ordained ecclesiastical norms, whether prompted by conscience or cussedness, posed no fundamental threat to public order. A far more serious incident took place, however, in 1577 as a result of the machinations of Sir Anthony Browne's great-nephew and heir, Wistan. Having disposed of Costed manor for £181 3s 4d, Wistan received a remission of a hundred pounds of the purchase price on condition of continuing to pay the five pounds annual salary of the chaplain of St Thomas's in Brentwood High Street. In fact Wistan was planning to do away with the chapel altogether. A petition sent on Brentwood's behalf to the Lord Keeper of the Great Seal alleged that Wistan Browne had taken away the chapel's seats and pews on 2 August. Three days later Thomasine Tyler (wife of the above John) led a mob of thirty women to surround the chapel and then "with force and arms they pulled a

certain Richard Brooke, schoolmaster, out of the said chapel and beat him, obstructing also the doors of the said chapel and locking themselves in the same, having and riotously using these arms: to wit, pitchforks, bills, a piked staff, two hot spits, three bows, nine arrows, one hatchet, one great hammer, hot water in two kettles, and a great sharp stone: and they kept themselves in the said chapel until they were arrested and removed...". There was clearly much local support for these Amazons. One local man, Henry Dalley, tried unsuccessfully to rescue Thomasine Tyler. Another local man refused to help the justices and Sheriff Wistan Browne. Seventeen of the women actually escaped arrest.

Within two days Wistan Browne was summoned to appear before the Privy Council and "in the meane while to forbeare the pulling downe of the chapell in Burntwoode." The Essex justices were subsequently ordered to free the women on bail and to impose only nominal fines of fourpence on them for form's sake, the Council having concluded that "the said Wistan Browne by his restraining of them from the use of the said chapell was the chiefest cause of the said force." It was left to the Court of High Commission to determine the status of the chapel and it concluded that Wistan Browne be compelled to restore it to full use. Wistan Browne's successor, another Sir Anthony Browne, was accused in 1616 of deliberately leaving the office of Brentwood's chaplain unfilled. The case was referred to the Exchequer Court and once again it was ordered that a chaplain should be instated with a house, orchard and an annual stipend of five pounds.

Sometimes 'religious controversy' was occasioned by motives even more transitory than greed. In the same year as the fracas at Brentwood chapel Thomas Smith, lord of the manor of Blackmore Priory, "with others openly in service time in the church made a brawl to the disquieting of the parson and the people gathered together, being then going to service." He pleaded that "by the means of others giving him occasion, there was high words." The judge accepted this as justifiable provocation. One law for the rich ....

MORALITY AND IMMORALITY

In 1581 Edward Maggett of Doddinghurst accused John Clement of hiding two whores in his house and of giving the constables free beer when they came to look for them in vain; Clement counter-claimed for slander. An Ingrave villager

47. *Elegant Doddinghurst rectory, representing the ordered calm of the eighteenth century – a striking contrast to the ecclesiastical turmoil of the preceding two centuries.*

accused a local tailor of keeping three such women secreted in separate houses. In 1583 Edmund Beare, a gentleman of Doddinghurst was accused of keeping a "defamed woman" in his house – neither of whom went to church.

In 1590 George Younge of Buttsbury was accused of adultery with Margaret Gubberd, wife of a Stock man. The accused produced eleven men to attest his innocence, only to have the woman confess to four transgressions with him in fields belonging to Sir John Petre. Apparently Younge had offered her fourpence for the first time – to which the offended husband responded with the observation that "Younge were better to give a hundred pounds than that Sir John Petre should know of his abuses" – but he would settle for ten shillings. Unfortunately for him the judge felt eleven supporters was enough to prove Younge innocent.

In 1592 an adulterous Brentwood man, having undergone penance, additionally offered to give a copy of Foxe's *Book of Martyrs* to South Weald Church or Brentwood chapel – which implies that neither then had one. (Emmison, doubtless

tongue in cheek but perhaps with rare mischievousness, suggests thefts by a devout Catholic.)

In 1593 William Carr of Ingatestone was accused of fornication by his own apprentice (apparently as a dare) – until the accuser was brought before Mr Mildmay JP and retracted everything. In the same year the wardens of East Horndon claimed but failed to prove that rector Robert Hunter was a bigamist. It was also alleged that "he giveth ill example of life by unquiet living, beating and chaining of his wife to a post and is a slanderer of his neighbours."

In 1597 the luckless William Wheeler of South Weald complained that "his wife used such company that he liked not of, and he often warned her to forbear and she would not" – but he was told to go on living with her as man and wife. In 1600 Clemence Bird of Ingatestone was excommunicated as "a very troublesome woman and a scolder among her neighbours". In the same year Jane Chapman, a widow of Childerditch, was excommunicated for remarrying in her own parlour.

In 1564 an East Horndon man who had taken

in a pregnant girl "for God's sake" was sentenced to public penance in the market and to pay two shillings to be given among the poor. In 1574 Hugh ap Harris of Mountnessing was arraigned for having harboured within his house a woman "great with child" married to "a sailor beyond the seas". These sound like acts of Christian charity. Neighbours would have been thinking of the applicability of another Act – a child born in a parish had the right to expect its support.

WITCHCRAFT

In the sixteenth and seventeenth centuries witchcraft was the second most common form of serious crime to be brought before Essex courts, exceeded only by theft. This reflects the fact that more accusations were brought in Essex than in any other county. Witchcraft had less to do with devil worship than with alleged malicious infliction of harm. In practice a distinction was drawn between that and what was perceived as 'white' witchcraft, intended to heal sickness or recover stolen property and which was treated as a spiritual misdemeanour, rather than a criminal offence, and dealt with accordingly. Considering its relative size Brentwood and its environs yielded fewer presentations for witchcraft than many smaller Essex settlements where, perhaps, rural isolation enabled social tensions to fester more malevolently. Nevertheless several instances are recorded and reflect the fact that the level of accusations generally reached a peak in the last quarter of the sixteenth century. In 1575 it was recorded that Julian Woodward of Brentwood "went to John Thomas a cunning man dwelling upon London Bridge for five shillings of money she lost and the same cunning man did show her in a glass a boy in a shirt gleaning corn resembling the countenance of John Hayes that had her money." Julian was dealt with lightly, being ordered only to do penance. The following year Joan, wife of Nicholas Baker, and Elizabeth Aylett, both of Brentwood, were accused of witchcraft. Similar accusations were levelled at Joan Symonde of Shenfield in 1580 and Alice Warren of Brentwood in 1597. One wonders what Alice's neighbours – or accusers – made of her death from plague the following year.

In 1600 Thomas Saye of Buttsbury was presented for having visited a local wizard to seek medicine for a sick child. He was discharged after being cautioned. In 1604 Katherine Weaver of Blackmore was charged with witchcraft but successfully pleaded in her defence that only one

48. *Essex witches depicted with the 'familiars' through which they allegedly communciated with the devil.*

churchwarden had brought the accusation and that he had been motivated by personal malice. She escaped with a caution.

Although the great majority of indictments were laid against females, men were not exempt. Charges were brought against George Burre of Brentwood in 1624 and Jane and Francis Lavender of Navestock in 1647, during the last major witch-hunting craze, which was largely confined to East Anglia.

Belief in the occult lingered on for decades yet. In April 1681 when the diarist Samuel Pepys was ill, his protégé Morelli, then living at Brentwood, wrote to inform him that if his illness persisted "there is a man here who can cure it if you please to send me down the pearings of the nailes of both your hands and foots and three locks of hair of the top of your crown I hope with the grace of God it will cure you."

PLURALISTS AND PURITANS

Samuel Harsnett (1561-1631), sometime rector of Shenfield, was a vigorous anti-Puritan and an unashamed pluralist who did at least use a part of his fortune to found Chigwell School. The son of a Colchester baker, he became a fellow of Pembroke Hall (now College), Cambridge before returning to the city of his birth as master of the free school. He soon abandoned "the painfull trade of teachyng" to return to Pembroke and deepen his studies in divinity. Having served as chaplain to Richard Bancroft, Bishop of London, Harsnett became vicar of Chigwell in 1597 and a prebend of St Paul's the following year.

As archdeacon of Essex from 1603 he published an anti-Catholic tract against the supposed power of casting out devils. Shakespeare evidently read it because he lifted from it the names of the spirits named by Edgar in *King Lear*. Harsnett became rector of Shenfield in 1604 and happily accepted the mastership of Pembroke the following year and the post of vice-chancellor of the university of Cambridge the year after that. He did resign his benefice at Chigwell in 1605 but in 1606 took up a compensatory appointment as vicar of Hutton. This he ceded to one of his own relatives, Adam Harsnett (died 1639) in 1609, the year in which he resigned his prebendal stall in favour of a nephew of Bancroft, by now Archbishop of Canterbury. (Adam managed to acquire the vicarage of Cranham, as well, and to retain both livings until his death.

Once again Samuel Harsnett was compensated for his timely gesture, receiving the rich living of Stisted, outside Braintree. In the same year he was made bishop of Chichester but allowed to retain Stisted. He was still Master of Pembroke but so much an absentee that the college accounts descended into chaos and the Fellows indicted him before James I on 57 counts. Harsnett was forced to resign but that did not stop him from proceeding to become bishop of Norwich and then archbishop of York and a privy councillor. A scourge of the Puritans, he gloried in ritual and, if high-handed and overbearing in his conduct

of office, was evidently a power in the pulpit, chosen by Bancroft himself to give his encomium. Given his predilection for liturgical display, it is ironic that Harsnett should, at his explicit request, have been buried at Chigwell with minimal ceremony, though memorialized with a fine brass.

John Childerley (1565-1645) was another pluralist, though far less successful than Harsnett. The son of a turner, he did not graduate as a Doctor of Divinity from Oxford until he was nearly forty. After ministering to the English merchant colony at Hamburg, Childerley, too, served Bancroft as a chaplain and managed to accumulate the preferments of St Mary Woolnoth and St Dunstan's-in-the-East in the City as well as the rectory of Shenfield, though the latter was sequestered from him by Parliament in 1643.

Nathaniel Ward (1578-1652), who held the Shenfield living from 1648 until his death, had, like Childerley served abroad – much further abroad. A product of that hothouse of Puritan divines, Emmanuel College, Cambridge, he was initially intended for the law and had also travelled as far as Switzerland and Denmark before belatedly taking holy orders at forty and, from 1620 to 1624, serving as chaplain to the British merchant colony at Elbing. Curate of St. James's, Piccadilly from 1626 to 1628, he was then presented to the rectory of Stondon Massey. Ward's puritan views brought him repeated reprimands from Archbishop Laud but he persisted in them until his dismissal in 1633. The following year he joined the 'Great Migration' to New England, settling at Agawam – later Ipswich – in Massachusetts. Resigning his ministry on health grounds in 1636, Ward then collaborated with the Rev. John Cotton of Boston to frame a 'Body of Liberties', the first legal code framed in New England. Ward was granted 600 acres near Pentucket – later renamed Haverhill after his birthplace – but he subsequently made this over to the infant college which became Harvard and returned to England in 1646.

Law and Disorder

IN THE OFFICE OF CONSTABLE

In Tudor England the enforcement of community obligations and the curbing of criminality rested almost entirely on the efforts of unpaid amateurs, of whom the parish constable bore the greatest burden. It was, understandably, an office few would gladly undertake, thankless, time-consuming, not infrequently hazardous and usually unpleasant. Constables routinely faced abuse in the course of discharging their duties. At Ingatestone they met "quarrelsome talk and unseemly words" and at Blackmore "opprobrious and threatening words" when confining a vagrant in the stocks. In 1588 two Brentwood blacksmiths gave "evil words" to a constable, having refused to shoe a mare he had brought to them. Sir John Petre and Edward Rich bound them over to observe more co-operative behaviour in the future.

Neighbourly solidarity sometimes prevailed over the obligations of office or social standing. In 1569 Francis Warner of Great Warley, a clerk (i.e. lower level priest) helped a parishioner assault the bailiff of the hundred (invariably unpopular as a low-level bully-boy) to rescue two horses, confiscated on a sheriff's warrant. In 1585 William Hollingsworth of Stondon Massey, gentleman, with three fellow villagers, beat up a sheriff's bailiff and took away his dagger to release Roger Parkyns, a Fryerning blacksmith. In 1588 Francis Smith, lord of the Priory manor of Blackmore, armed with a drawn sword, struck the constable at the church-gate and released John Reve, a local mercer and ale-house keeper whom the constable had confined in the church. It was a risky enterprise, attacks in a church or churchyard carrying a statutory punishment of the loss of an ear or branding of a cheek. In 1589 Charles Smyth, gentleman, of Blackmore, with two yeomen, assaulted a deputy constable of Blackmore to release a prisoner arrested on suspicion of felony. Smyth, although probably the son of the lord of the manor, fled nevertheless, perhaps because he was also accused of horse-stealing that same year.

49. Low levels of detection encouraged reliance on deterrence. A malefactor is flogged to the gallows while respectable citizens look on approvingly. Illustration from Hollinshed's Chronicles.

50. *A beggar's plea for alms is ignored, illustrated in 1569.*

THE GAME OF THE GAME

Neighbourliness was enjoined on all as a Christian as well as a civic virtue.

The perennially troublesome were liable to end up before the justices. In 1564 John Pattryke, a yeoman of Ingrave, was indicted by his neighbours as

"a very troublous and disordered person of evil name, fame and conversation, a common quarreller among us and other our neighbours, a railer against such as be honest of the parish, in calling them thieves, villains and other odible names of reproach and infamy, daily seeking and procuring by false lies and devices of his busy brain to set variance and strifes between the parishioners."

Pattryke had been up before the bench the previous year for poaching rabbits by stretching nets across "an ancient lane called Chick House Garden"and another called Drudgells Lane, both in Ingrave, being fined twelve pence for the first offence and twenty for the second. In 1565 he was up on the same charge again, Drudgells Lane costing him forty pence. It appears to have been something of a family weakness. In 1582 James Pattryke, husbandman, with three others, pitched a trap on Ingrave Common between one and two in the morning, taking four rabbits. When they tried to set the trap a second time they were challenged by Sir John Petre's warrener and assistants and a scuffle ensued. Pattryke was fined ten pounds, making his nocturnal excursion a particularly expensive one. For Petre's warrener it was the second successful prosecution in a month, having nabbed brickmaker Geoffrey Lorken of East Horndon for the same offence in the same place.

Poaching not only put meat in a poor man's pot, it was also a challenge widely enjoyed. An indictment of 1565 bound over no less than fifteen men, mostly of Great Warley. Matthew Pery, a gentleman of the same parish was charged separately with using both a crossbow and a handgun; poor men used nets or snares. The desire to poach efficiently led to further crimes, thus feeding on itself. In 1575 two men stole four sparrowhawks, valued at four pounds from a Mountnessing wood. In 1585 two Margaretting men and a yeoman from Great Baddow were confronted in West Horndon Park by Sir John Petre's keeper and found to be in possession of ten sparrowhawks, having broken into the Petre mews. A fight ensued. One at least of the perpetrators was gaoled.

Poaching was not invariably motivated by poverty or class resentment. An element of 'dare' may have inspired Thomas Crane, a gentleman of Navestock to break into the Queen's park at Havering and kill two male deer with a 'birding-piece'. Arthur Tappes of Blackmore, gentleman, likewise poached a stag in the Petre park at Writtle. Francis Chaunsey of Shenfield, gentleman, was fined twenty pence for taking rabbits from the lands of his neighbour, Thomas Parker. Does that nominal fine reflect the humiliation of being fined or a wink at a prank? Almost a century later Sir John Bramston reminisced how when he had been a schoolboy at Blackmore around 1630 his master had encouraged pupils to eke out their scanty rations by poaching his neighbours' doves.

ROBBERY AND BURGLARY

The volume of traffic passing along the Essex Great Road made highway robbery an obvious temptation. When Christopher Rudding was riding near Brentwood at four in the morning in November 1567 a band of robbers jumped from cover by the roadside, bundled him up with two sacks, threw him in a wayside ditch and got away with just under thirty pounds. The victim was able to name two of his assailants but, although they were caught and brought to trial, they were found not guilty. Shortly before Christmas 1587 two separate robberies took place at Ingatestone, the first victim losing 24s 8d, his cloak and his knife, the second four shillings and his knife. The culprits may have been discharged seamen.

Normally violence seems to have been rare in these encounters. The fact that only sixty-five cases led to indictments for highway robbery in all of Essex over the course of Elizabeth's long reign implies that most people knew that the chance of an arrest and successful prosecution was so minimal that they simply accepted their losses and let the matter drop.

Local records provide evidence of housebreaking targeted on high-profile members of the community, usually by malefactors from outside it, often well outside. In 1586 a labourer from Stock broke into the house of Thomas Smith Esquire at the former Blackmore Priory, carrying away valuable silver-gilt items including a salt-cellar, pepper-box and tankard, two silver spoons and a pound and a half of woollen yarn. He was found not guilty for taking the plate but fined ten pence for the yarn. Considering that he had been acquitted for burgling another house in Blackmore eight years earlier this lenience remains to be explained. George White, owner of Hutton Hall, was at home and so were his servants when in 1591 a Chelsea labourer broke in and tried to make off with whatever he could grab – a carpet valued at twenty shillings and a history of the Italian wars in French, valued at just sixteen pence. In 1600 Thoby Priory, the Mountnessing home of John Butler, a JP, was likewise burgled while the owner and his household were there. Two Margaretting women were charged with stealing shirts and linen to the value of £9 13s 4d from the house but were subsequently acquitted. In the same year four men had the temerity to break into Weald Hall itself, carrying away a cover, cushion, canopy, carpets and curtains of silk and taffeta, valued at over thirty pounds.

Thieves were sometimes caught and dealt with severely. Two Purfleet watermen who broke into a Shenfield house in 1597, carrying off £9 10s worth of booty, were hanged for it.

FORCE MAJEURE

Although Ingatestone Hall was built with crenellations these were probably decorative rather than defensive. Yet, despite the good order supposedly imposed by the Tudors, instances of 'disseisin', the violent seizure of properties, continued to occur even in Essex, so close to the capital. At least eighteen cases took place under Mary and a further sixty spread throughout the supposedly more settled reign of Elizabeth. As the properties involved were often substantial the leaders were usually from the supposedly respectable rather than the criminal classes, although the latter were often enlisted as muscle. In 1561 William Bradbourne Esquire acquired the manor of Myles in Kelvedon Hatch by right of marriage. The following year Reginald Hollingsworth, gentleman, aided by Lawrence and William, yeomen of the same name, all of Stondon Massey, combined to evict Bradbourne.

In 1568 John Tyrrell was forcibly ejected from Little Warley Hall by four local yeomen backed by a band of armed but unknown men. There appears to have been a family quarrel behind this as the instigator was Ludovick/Lewis Greville, son-in-law of Sir William Petre, whose second wife had originally been married to a Tyrrell. Restitution was successfully effected by the processes of the law. In 1596 the same property was attacked by a gang of Londoners, but presumably with a view to plunder rather than seizure.

In 1571 Thomas Veere, occupying Childerditch Hall as tenant of the widowed Lady Anne Maltravers, was dispossessed by ten local men and women. They were all fined a paltry fourpence but their thirty-plus accomplices, who were not successfully identified, presumably went unpunished. In 1579 a London silk weaver and four others broke into the Rectory at Kelvedon Hatch by night "intending to murder and plunder the rector and his wife." In 1594 Richard Lovelace, a tenant, was forcibly ejected from Loft Hall, Navestock by Thomas Carowe, gentleman, with the aid of three local labourers.

Modern research suggests that the homicide rate in early modern England was at least six times as high as it is nowadays. Most men routinely carried a dagger and went more heavily armed when travelling. The will of Thomas Ellkinge, possibly a retainer of the Tyrrell family, included bequests to fellow servants of "one rapier and a dagger which I have lying at Ingatestone ... and ... one long sword, a gauntlet and a dagger which be in my chamber in Mill Green at Fryerning."

Considering that Brentwood was so close to the nation's seat of government and justice, rather than in some border wasteland, lethal incidents involving local residents are noteworthy for their brutality, if not their frequency. Thomas Winckfield of Brentwood (gentleman!) stabbed a London spinster in the buttock so viciously that she died; he fled. A Navestock sawyer hit a maidservant on the head with his axe, fled but

51. *The Assize House at Brentwood. Note the whipping-post to the right. The stocks stood at the rear.*

later confessed. Thomas Foster, gentleman, arrested under a writ by sheriff's bailiffs near Romford, was rescued by an armed gang when passing through South Weald. One of the bailiffs was killed by a rapier thrust. Surprisingly in view of the death of a law officer, the rescuer and Foster were found guilty of homicide but not murder. At Tiptree Gilbert Hyndes of Brentwood, yeoman, attacked Ralph Elzynge of Little Horkesley with his sword, killing him, but claimed self-defence.

The successful detection of criminals was, in the absence of any regular police forces, inevitably haphazard. But some officers of the law used its not inconsiderable weight to get results.

In 1581 a jury declared to the coroner that its members "knew nothing" regarding the unexplained death of a South Weald widow. Judging them wilfully recalcitrant, the coroner threatened them with a fine of five pounds – each. Thus prompted, they suddenly remembered that the luckless victim had had her throat cut in her own house, with her own scissors, by local labourer John in le Winde, who had, unsurprisingly, fled. Edward Pynchon, gentleman, of Writtle, had less luck when, accompanied by a constable and armed with a warrant from John Butler J.P., he tried to arrest a man in Thomas Tabor's inn at Brentwood. The customers rose as a body against him and the innkeeper's brother choked him half to death.

Coaching Days

The role of Brentwood and Ingatestone in catering for travellers long pre-dates the emergence of turnpiked roads and regular coaching services in the later seventeenth century. Pilgrims bound for Canterbury and passengers bound to or from the Continent via Harwich provided two constant sources of legitimate custom. There was also the unlawful kind. In 1468 a tenant at Heybregge (Heybridge) was ordered to cut back an overgrown pasture bordering the king's highway "for that robbers lurk there by day and night to despoil passers-by." Records of the Court of Chancery document the case *c.*1483 of a wretched Colchester merchant who, returning home from business in London, was robbed of his documentation by "certain evil disposed persons unknown to him at the town of Brentwood" and was consequently desperate to prove that he had not been involved in some criminal deception.

Brentwood's White Hart, George, Bell, Crown and Chequers inns all dated back to at least the fifteenth or early sixteenth centuries. In 1556 presentments were brought against a further six unlicensed ale-houses in the town and in 1567 it was alleged that a Shenfield butcher "keepeth an alehouse and doth daily hospitate and succour vagabonds and idle persons and suffer them to play at cards." A Brentwood man was similarly indicted for harbouring "all manner of lewd and wandering persons." Local drunks and gamesters, their nuisance value being a known quantity, were more tolerable than "sturdy beggars" from nowhere who might present a serious threat to local property or even lives. Besides which, habitual drunkenness mattered less in itself than the violence, vice or idleness it implied, hence presentments before the justices such as "John Harris alias Black John of Blackmore liveth out of service and lieth at an alehouse very suspiciously, for that he hath nothing to live on and hath there remained a year or thereabouts ".

Neighbours could denounce but they could also provide support. In 1590 John Abell of Mountnessing got eight friends to sign a 'certificate' petitioning the justices that he might open an ale-house – "the place where he dwelleth is meet for that purpose and the man of honest behaviour."

Brentwood's growing prosperity meant that it had eleven licensed houses in 1578. There were

52. A tavern scene in Stuart times. Inns brought prosperity to Brentwood and Ingatestone, creating employment for servants, ostlers, cooks and laundresses, as well as suppliers of food, drink and fodder.

also two more at South Weald and Brook Street. The town's importance was recognised in 1579 by the building of an Assize House for "Justices of the Assize to keep the Assizes and gaol delivery in." Behind the Assize House *(ill. 51)* was the market place where the town's stocks, whipping post and cage were located. A gibbet stood at Gallows Green at the junction of the Ongar and Doddinghurst Roads.

By 1600 the town had a population of six to seven hundred, living in some ninety houses, most ranged along the High Street and Back (Hart) Street. The marginal growth of population which was normal in most years was savagely checked on occasion by epidemic outbreaks. In the plague year of 1625 fifty souls were born but ninety-two buried. In the year of London's Great Plague, 1664-5, 76 births were offset by 98 deaths.

A MORE THAN NINE DAYS' WONDER

It is perhaps a tribute to the importance of the Essex Great Road and the populousness and prosperity of the region through which it passed that in 1599 the famous actor Will Kemp announced that he would morris-dance all the way to Norwich, in preference to, say, Dover or Bristol. Kemp, accompanied by his servant, a tabour player and an 'overseer' to detect any attempt at cheating, was seen off by a crowd gathered outside the Lord Mayor's residence in London and made his way over Bow Bridge out through Stratford and Ilford to Romford, where he rested for two days. Projected as a 'Nine Days Wonder' the journey actually took twenty-three, reflecting Kemp's entrepreneurial shrewdness in timing

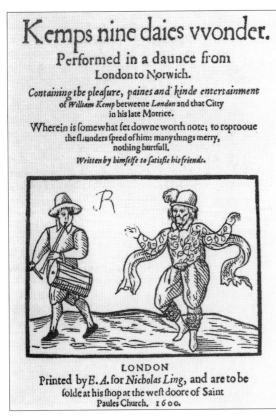

53. Will Kemp on his dancing marathon. He carefully timed his entrance to Brentwood to coincide with market day.

his appearances to maximum effect. (His servant also carried a stock of gloves, garters and knick-knacks to sell along the way.) Kemp therefore took care to pass through Brentwood on a Thursday because it was market day. "I roused myself and ... so merrily to Burnt Wood ... The Multitudes were so great at my coming ... that I had much ado (though I made many entreaties and stays) to get passage to my inn."

Further, unexpected publicity was gained by the fortuitous arrest of two 'cutpurses' who, with two further accomplices, had followed Kemp all the way from London, doubtless hoping to find easy pickings among yokels drawn to gawp at the much-heralded spectacle of a lunatic Londoner capering along the Queen's Highway. Apprehended, the two villains tried to bluster their way out of trouble by claiming that they had laid bets on Kemp and had simply tagged along to safeguard their investment. Their bluff was readily called – "the Officers bringing them to

my Inn I justly denied their acquaintance, saying that I remembered one of them to be a noted culpurse, such a one as we tie to a post on our stage, for all people to wonder at when at a play they are taken pilfering. This fellow and his halfbrother ... were sent to jayle; their other two consorts had the charity of the town and after a dance ... at the whipping cross, they were sent back to London." After resting Kemp went on his way "... the moon shining clearly and the weather being calm, in the evening, I tripped into Ingerstone." He did eventually reach Norwich where the Lord Mayor laid on a triumphal welcome and gave him a bounty of five pounds and a life pension of forty shillings.

INNS AND TURNPIKES

As early as 1622 there were complaints emanating from Chelmsford about the damage done to the road to Brentwood by heavy cart traffic which had rendered the thoroughfare "exceeding ruinous for six to seven miles, with deep sloughs, pits, and holes, very harmful to all passengers on horses and dangerous to the overthrow of coach, waggon or cart." Local justices reckoned that repairs would cost the very substantial sum of £500 and recommended a ban on heavy waggons from 1 October to 30 April each year. A more positive comment of 1636 noted that Ingatestone offered "excellent neat entertainment to travellers". Brentwood's first named postmaster, Samuel Smith, is recorded in 1637 and was paid an annual salary of five pounds a year, as were his successors for over a century. The intensification of commerce supported a diversification of the local economy into specialised manufactures and services. Brewers and maltsters are recorded in Brentwood from the early seventeenth century. By 1657 there was a feltmaker and a little later collar-makers. In 1667 an apothecary and an attorney are recorded. By 1678 fairs were being held twice a year, from 7th to 9th July and 4th to 6th October. Between 1670 and 1690 the number of houses in Brentwood rose by eleven per cent.

In 1686 it was reckoned that Brentwood's inns could muster between them 110 beds and stabling for 183 horses. This suggests commercial enterprise on a considerable scale but not perhaps necessarily to the highest standards. When Mary, Countess of Warwick, en route from London to Leighs, stayed overnight in Brentwood she found the experience positively purgatorial:

54. *A dispute over the bill in a tavern in Stuart times.*

"With what cheerfulness and serenity of mind did I bear with all the inconveniences and ill entertainment of this inn, upon this consideration, that what I met with there was not to last, but at night, when I came home to my own house, I should have abundant recompense made me by the good things I should there enjoy. O, my soul, turn this into spiritual advantage and consider that all the ill entertainment I meet with in this vain world is but the ill accommodations of this great Inn ...".

The first Act of Parliament relating to the improvement of roads in Essex dates from 1695 and incidentally used the word 'turnpike' in a statute for the first time. It provided for the repair of several sections of the road out to Harwich,

including the stretch between 'Shenfield and Ingatestone Town'. Funds for the upkeep of the road were to be derived from tolls paid by users at a gate to be erected "at or near Mountnessing." In 1711 coaches ran from London to Harwich twice a week. The journey time was normally a day and a half, although a petition from Shenfield in 1715 complained that the road could be impassable in winter. From 1721 onwards the section of road passing through Brook Street was upgraded by the Middlesex and Essex Turnpike Trust and in 1725 a further Turnpike Act was passed to upgrade the section from Shenfield through Ingatestone to Chelmsford. Daniel Defoe, writing his *Tour Through the Whole Island of Great*

55. Daniel Defoe. The writer was also a businessman with a tile-making works at Tilbury.

no Road in England can yet be said to equal them; this was first done by the help of a Turnpike, set up by Act of Parliament, about the year 1697, at a Village near Ingerstone ... The first Toll near Ingerstone, being the highest rated public Toll in England ..."

No matter, such being the benefit to traffic that

"the gentlemen of the County, design to petition the Parliament, to have the Commissioners ... empowered to place other Turnpikes, on the other most Considerable Roads, and so to Undertake and Repair all the Roads in the whole County...".

ALWAYS WITH YOU ...

The vigorous commerce generated by the improved road system did not, of course, imply the banishment of poverty. Age, illness and ill fortune inevitably condemned a proportion of the populace to penury and reliance on the organised compassion of their parish. The house of one Daniel Barnard in Ingrave Road was hired as a workhouse. A South Weald couple, Robert Maxwell and his wife, were hired "to keep 'em all in good order ... and ... for such their good services ... be allow'd four shillings a week, together with their dyet and lodging in the said house. "

Being so near London and on a major highway Brentwood was potentially liable to attract paupers ejected from the capital. The overseers of the poor doubtless devoted much of their time to detecting them and moving them on to become a burden on some less vigilant community. The obligation to care for those with a right to a 'settlement' in a parish cut two ways. In 1737 Mr Foster, a Brentwood overseer, went all the way to Kendal to try to persuade the authorities there to accept responsibility for a Brentwood man, Edward Beck, who had settled there. The journey took twenty-four days. Foster was allowed two shillings a day for expenses but, as an overseer, would have been unpaid and presumably undertook this odyssey at the expense of his own affairs. Service as overseer of the poor was the most onerous of parish offices and perhaps this explains why there were always two and in large parishes up to four and the term of office was limited to six months. In 1801 a Blackmore farmer defying "every remonstrance" from the local magistrate was fined five pounds and gaoled for two months for his refusal to serve. Even the illiterate were not exempt. At Stondon Massey a rota of farmers was drawn up in advance so that they could know when their term was due and plan accordingly.

Britain at this very time, referred to Brentwood, Ingatestone and Chelmsford as "large thoroughfare towns, full of good inns, and chiefly maintained by the excessive multitude of carriers and passengers, which are constantly passing this way to London, with droves of cattle, provisions and manufactures". The dynamic impact of the capital's immense concentrated purchasing power on England's various regional economies provided a constant motif running through Defoe's observations. With ten per cent of the nation's entire population and a significantly high proportion of its disposable wealth London generated a seemingly insatiable demand for products and people, made visibly manifest by the throngs of coaches and waggons which travelled the Essex Great Road.

Defoe was emphatic about the revolution which turnpikes had effected in a single generation:

"These roads were formerly deep, in time of Floods dangerous, and at other times, in Winter, scarce passable; they are now so firm, so safe, so easy to Travellers, and carriages as well as Cattle, that

56. *An eighteenth-century coaching map of the Essex Great Road.*

FASTER AND FASTER

In 1747 the road from the Eagle & Child at Shenfield out to Billericay and Rayleigh was also turnpiked. Increased traffic created its own temptations. In 1750 Thomas Munn 'gentleman brickmaker' of Brentwood was hanged for robbing the Yarmouth mail and his corpse hanged in chains at Gallows Corner. In 1785 George Ingram of Shenfield was hanged for horse-stealing.

By the 1760s there was a regular daily coach service via Brentwood running from the Black Bull on Bishopsgate in London to the Great White Horse at Ipswich, total journey time ten hours. In 1770 the Chelmsford Machine Fly began as an additional passenger service to London.

Improvements in road surfacing and the accelerating expansion of the British economy after the disruptions of the American war for independence led to a further rapid expansion of commerce and accompanying traffic. A London-Norwich mail coach service was inaugurated in 1785 and ran for the next sixty years. By 1791 there were no less than three daily coach services from Brentwood to London, plus a waggon service for goods and non-premium passengers four times a week. In 1793 it was assumed that letters despatched at 5am would be delivered in London the same day, the standard charge being four pence. Journey times improved significantly. At mid-century it took five and a half hours to go from London to Chelmsford, by the end of the century, when four companies were operating the route, only four hours. The names of the coaches reflected their status as kings of the road – the Ipswich Quicksilver and Norwich Phenomena, the Light Chelmsford, Colchester Defiance, Yarmouth Star and Tally-Ho. The drivers, too, were often celebrated 'characters', known by dashing soubriquets. George Palmer was 'Brandy George' while John Murrell, who clearly took a rather different view of his responsibilities was 'Drinkwater Jack'.

OUTS AND INNS

If Brentwood and Ingatestone were bustling with commercial life, their satellite settlements remained somnolent and overwhelmingly rural. Childerditch, which had just 32 houses in 1670, still had only forty by 1766. Britain's first census, conducted in 1801, reckoned its population at just 188 souls. Great Warley in 1671 had only 59

57. A grand private equipage outside Old Mill Green House, Fryerning.

58. The George and Dragon after the demise of the coaching trade.

houses, although a number of these were quite substantial, sixteen having six hearths or more. By 1801 the village had 430 inhabitants. Growth was more marked in roadside villages. The number in Mountnessing rose from 40 in 1723 to 85 in 1801.

In 1788 Brentwood had eleven inns, ten ranged along the High Street, plus the Robin Hood (now Robin Hood and Little John) on the Ongar Road. Of these four are still extant – the White Hart, Lion and Lamb (formerly Lamb), Swan (formerly Gun) and White Horse. The Crown then adjoined St Thomas's chapel on the London side and in 1793 served as the post office. In 1797 it kept three post chaises and thirteen post horses. Adjoining the chapel on the other side was the Chequers. The other inns were the Ship (aka Yorkshire Grey), the Marquis of Granby, the George (aka George and Dragon), which was already in existence by 1407 and traded till *c*.1906, and the Bell, which traded from at least 1454 until *c*.1951. Although the Crown had closed by 1818 and the Marquis of Granby by 1829, the King's Head, a former inn

which had gone out of business by 1788, reopened in 1826.

That coaching inns were substantial operations can be judged from the fact that an intending landlord of the Rose and Crown was expected to have a minimum capital of a hundred guineas, while the stock of one Ingatestone inn was put at two hundred and fifty pounds in 1795.

In 1838 a single day's traffic through the Shenfield tollgate included 176 coaches and carriages, 24 post horses, 13 saddle horses, 2,120 sheep and 1,110 cattle. By 1839, the year before the railway reached Brentwood, the town was linked by regular coach services not only along the main through route to London, Chelmsford and Harwich but also to Ipswich, Bury St Edmunds, Norwich and Southend.

The coaching inns of Brentwood and Ingatestone generated a steady demand for beer, some at least of which was locally supplied. In the first decade of the nineteenth century Tabor and Jaggard had a brewhouse at Fryerning. Brentwood's White Hart was a tied house controlled by Ongar brewer George Williams.

The concentration of inns in Brentwood and Ingatestone probably helped to keep standards of service up as disgruntled travellers could exercise the prerogative of choice and go elsewhere. A Suffolk gentleman who travelled frequently to London in the 1780s complimented an establishment in Ingatestone for a dinner of "very fine mackerel and cutlets" and a lunch of whiting and veal. Arriving in the town late on a stormy night he was delighted to find that chicken and tarts were still available. The Red Lion at Ingatestone kept a canal stocked full of fresh fish for diners.

The regular business of inns was catering to the needs of travellers, serving as meeting-places for the conduct of local business and providing facilities for social intercourse. (There was a gentlemen's club meeting at the White Hart in Brentwood by 1713.) But sometimes the recreation often incidental to these purposes became temporarily the main business itself. In March 1789 the yard of the Swan at Ingatestone witnessed a celebrated pugilistic encounter between 'Gentleman' John Jackson (1769-1845) of London and George 'the Brewer' Ingleston of Ilford. Jackson had made his first public appearance in June of the previous year near Croydon, defeating Fewterell of Birmingham in the presence of the Prince of Wales in a contest lasting sixty-seven minutes. The Ingatestone encounter was to prove much briefer. The boards, set up in the yard to serve as a ring, had been soaked by an overnight shower, making them slippery. Jackson's superior skill soon became evident as the Brewer was knocked down and by the third round the Ilford man was clearly being outclassed. But then Jackson slipped awkwardly, dislocating his ankle and fracturing a leg bone. The injured man then made the bizarre if sporting offer to continue, tied to a chair. Ingleston, having secured the purse, not unnaturally declined. Jackson's third and final fight, at Hornchurch in 1795, saw him beat Mendoza the Jew in ten and a half minutes to replace him as champion of England. Retiring in 1803, he opened a fashionable boxing academy in Bond Street, where Byron became a friend and ardent admirer. At the coronation of his former patron as George IV Jackson organised a team of eighteen other prize-fighters dressed as pages to keep the riff-raff out of the Abbey.

Cricket was another attraction favoured by publicans as a means of attracting a thirsty crowd.

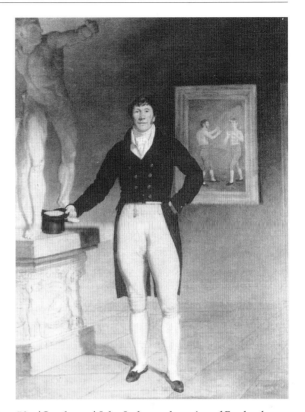

59. 'Gentleman' John Jackson, champion of England 1795-1803. Oil painting by Ben Marshall, 1810

The New Inn at Ingatestone organised a match against a team from Gravesend for a purse of fifty pounds staked by the players. Cricket was also played at Navestock's Green Man. The racegoers on Warley Common were catered for by The Crown at Brentwood, which also put on concerts in its Great Ballroom. In 1796 the Hounslow Company of Comedians put on *School for Scandal* at Brentwood's Lion and Lamb.

The coming of the railway did not lead to the immediate demise of the coaching trade. A new business opened up to take advantage of the limited extent of the existing network, with coaches bringing passengers from Braintree and Witham via Chelmsford to take trains from Brentwood up to London. The respite could only be temporary. By 1843 the line had reached Colchester. The last run of the Yarmouth Star was driven by its veteran coachman, Fiddler Dring, who boasted that he had slept alternate nights in London and Norwich for half a century. At the corner of Love Lane and Queens Road the coach overturned, killing the driver.

Alarms and Excursions

CIVIL WAR

When civil war broke out between king and parliament in 1642 it was at Brentwood that the Earl of Warwick initially mustered five hundred men in support of the parliamentary cause. The eastern counties were fairly solidly for Parliament and Essex in particular was held by puritans to be the "place of most life of religion in the land." Nevertheless there were numerous royalist supporters in the area – Sir John Lucas of Shenfield, Colonel John Browne and Sir Anthony Browne IV of South Weald, Sir Denner Strutt of Little Warley Hall and Sir John Tyrrell of East Horndon, whose epitaph bore witness to the price he paid for his loyalty: "Upon him once decimated, twice imprisoned, thrice sequestered, he holds his peace as oft as plundered". Sir Edward Waldegrave of Navestock commanded a royalist regiment of horse with distinction and was rewarded with a baronetcy in 1643. Sir Anthony Browne's loyalty plunged him into such debt that he was eventually to be obliged to sell Weald Hall to the mendacious lawyer William Scroggs. Ralph Pettus of Brizes at Kelvedon had his estate sequestrated and was unable to raise the eight hundred pounds needed to redeem it.

The learned Samuel Baker, Vicar of South Weald, was replaced by the Puritan Nicholas Folkingham and subsequently imprisoned. Folkingham was followed by Thomas Goodwin, a fellow of St John's College, Cambridge, "a person of great learning, exemplary piety and universal reputation", who also held the living of Brentwood.

Brentwood saw little direct evidence of conflict until the second phase of the civil wars in June 1648 when a royalist force under the Earl of Norwich crossed from Kent and marched from Bow along the Essex Great Road, hoping to recruit further supporters en route. At Brentwood they were joined by a contingent led by Sir Charles Lucas, a dashing royalist cavalry commander who had twice been captured by Parliamentary forces and had given his parole not to take up arms against them again. The royalists, by now some five thousand strong, pressed on up to Colchester, pursued by a parliamentary body of troops under Colonel Whalley and Sir Thomas Fairfax.

The outcome was a long and bloody siege, ending in the capitulation of the royalist garrison and the summary execution of Lucas.

In 1649 the wealthy dilettante and diarist John Evelyn bought the manor of Great Warley. Although he attended meetings of the manorial court assiduously he chose not to live there and sold it on in 1655 because "the taxes are so intolerable that they eat up the rents etc. surcharged as that county has been during our unnatural war."

In 1657 Cromwell's Physician-in-Ordinary, Lawrence Wright (1590-1657) was buried at St Peter's, South Weald. Born near Hornchurch, he had studied medicine at Cambridge and Leyden before rising steadily through the ranks of the Royal College of Physicians, being admitted in 1618, elected fellow in 1624 and serving as a member of its council for the last decade of his life. Wright was also chosen as physician to Sir Thomas Sutton's newly-established London charity, a combined school and retirement home, at the Charterhouse, of which he eventually became Governor. Wright married the daughter of a fellow Essex physician, had two sons and acquired property at Henham and Havering. It was probably unfortunate for Cromwell, who died of "a bastard tertian ague" – possibly some form of malaria – that Wright predeceased him. Whether Wright could have done better than the physicians who succeeded him we can never know, though he would certainly have known the patient longer and had already seen him successfully through two serious illnesses. That Wright was held in esteem we may reasonably assume from the fact that Cromwell created his younger son a baronet.

PEPYS, PLAGUE AND PLOTTERS

Evelyn's friend and fellow diarist Samuel Pepys (1633-1703) had what one might call a necessarily passing acquaintance with Brentwood, as his duties as a naval administrator periodically took him to Harwich, for which he was also twice MP. But he was also in Brentwood on a number of occasions for more personal reasons. In July 1665 he played the part of go-between in respect of a proposed marriage between Lt Philip Carteret of *HMS Royal Oak*, son of Pepys's boss, Sir George Carteret, Treasurer of the Navy, and Lady Jemimah Montague, daughter of the Earl of Sandwich, Pepys's patron. Pepys accompanied the prospective groom to meet the prospective bride at Dagnams, an estate of her aunt, Lady

60. *Samuel Pepys, the member of Parliament for Harwich*

Wright, at Noak Hill, between Brentwood and Romford. Pepys was irritated by Carteret's ineptitude and the girl's bashfulness but must have been relieved when she promised to obey her parents and make the match. Pepys returned on the last day of the month, too late for the service but still in time for the feast.

While plague raged in London at that time, Pepys was amused to witness a rather bizarre incident. A maidservant, sick of the plague, had escaped an outhouse to which she had been confined and was found wandering distractedly. Consigned to a specially designated pest-coach to be returned to confinement behind closed curtains, she was waylaid in a narrow lane by Sir Anthony Browne, his brother and some of their friends:

"The brother being a young man and believing there might be some lady in it that would not be seen ... he thrust his head ... into her coach and to look, and there saw somebody very ill ... and stunk mightily ... which put the young gentleman into a fright had almost cost him his life..."

Brentwood figured in another Pepysian episode at the time of the 'Popish Plot' when Pepys's personal loyalty to his former master, the openly Catholic Duke of York, caused his own allegiance to be called in question. Pepys was confined to the Tower of London in May 1679 on patently absurd and malicious charges of treasonable correspondence with France, plotting to extirpate Protestantism ... It was further claimed in support of these accusations that one Cesare Morelli, a Flemish Catholic music-master who had lodged in the Pepys household for a while, was actually a Jesuit priest in disguise. At no little expense Pepys had already had him spirited away to live discreetly under cover in Brentwood with a Mr and Mrs Slater. Charges were eventually dropped and Pepys was released after finding a huge surety. One of Pepys's former servants subsequently made a deathbed confession that he had made up the accusations after being bribed by one of Pepys's enemies, William Harbord, MP for Thetford. Morelli stayed on in Brentwood and Pepys came out to visit him in September 1680 and again in August 1681.

The Popish Plot had an even less happy outcome for William, fourth Lord Petre (1627-83). As a prominent practising Catholic he fell under suspicion and was imprisoned in the Tower. Claiming vociferously to be the victim of "a false and injurious calumny", he petitioned the King repeatedly for his release. In his final letter he declared that "with my last breath I beg of God to defend your Majesty from all your enemies and to forgive those who by their perjuries have endeavoured to make me appear to be one." Charles II remained deaf to these pleas and Petre died in the Tower after a confinement of five years.

Another casualty of the Popish Plot – much to his surprise – was the lord chief justice William Scroggs (?1623-83) who had purchased the manor of South Weald from those Brownes whose royalist loyalties had cost them dear. A butcher's son, an ex-captain of royalist infantry, a rake and boon companion of Charles II, Scroggs was also a forceful and persuasive advocate. But he was none too scrupulous in matters of truth and his willing acceptance of the perjured testimony of Titus Oates against alleged anti-royalist plotters was therefore all the more nauseating. Vigorously browbeating or flattering juries as it served his purpose, Scroggs enthusiastically despatched a procession of alleged traitors to the scaffold. His abuses became so blatant that eventually he was impeached before the Lords but the dissolution of parliament led to the charges being dropped.

Scroggs had, however, become so hated that it was deemed prudent to dismiss him from the bench, though a pension of £1500 doubtless sweetened the pill as the reviled judge withdrew to a sulky retirement at South Weald. He used his remaining years to revise the reports of the thirteen state trials over which he had presided, selling his versions to London publishers to augment his bloated income still further.

IN CAMP

Troops are known to have camped on Warley Common in 1742 during the war of Austrian Succession and by 1759 the site was sufficiently well established for this purpose for a schedule of "rules to be observed by persons visiting Warley camp" to be issued.

In the summer of 1778 a major muster of troops took place there. The rebellion in the American colonies had won the support of France and once again there was a fear of a French invasion. Expectations of well-honed military precision were not universal. The former Mary Martin, by then married to Isaac Rebow, then serving with the militia congregated at Warley, wrote, evidently in response to his reassurances, "I am very pleased there is no time for the bottle, for, as you know my opinion of some of your party, it relieves some of my fears ...".

George III came down in person to Warley to review soldiers who had come from as far away as Yorkshire. Dr Samuel Johnson also came, staying for five days with a captain of the Lincolnshire militia, Bennet Langton. Johnson, who once observed that "every man thinks meanly of himself for not having been a soldier ", was, despite his advancing years, still keenly interested in military affairs. Warley gave him the opportunity to watch Langton preside over a court-martial (for sheep-stealing), do the rounds of the night picket, admire the musketry of the militiamen and quiz the officers about gunpowder, the weight of musket balls and the effective range of different weapons. Johnson also dined with General Hall, the officer commanding, who graciously pronounced himself honoured by the occasion. Another visitor to Warley was the exiled Corsican patriot Pascal Paoli, who had become a close friend of Johnson and a courtier to George III. The encampment was also considered sufficiently memorable to be depicted in two pictures by Philip de Loutherburg.

Warley camp continued in existence into the

61. *Dr Samuel Johnson spent five days at Warley Camp.*

autumn for we find Johnson writing solicitously on 31 October to his erstwhile host Langton: "When are you to be cantoned in better habitations? The air grows cold and the ground damp. Longer stay in the camp cannot be without much danger to the health of the common men, if even the officers can escape." By the following month Langton and his men had moved on to Hertfordshire. There was, however, more to fear than cold and damp. The parish register of Great Warley for 1778 records the death of a duellist.

After reviewing the troops at Warley George III and Queen Charlotte went to stay with the Petres at Thorndon Hall. Their host, Robert Edward, ninth baron Petre (1742-1801) had been a major moving spirit behind the Catholic Relief Act passed that year to ease the civil disabilities of adherents to the Roman church. A royal visit appeared to set the seal of approval on his efforts. It was allegedly the first visit paid to the home of a practising Catholic by a reigning monarch since the Reformation. Two days of hospitality set the host back more than £1100. In 1780 Petre further had the satisfaction of being elected a Fellow of the Society of Antiquaries and a Fellow of the Royal Society.

62 & 63. *Warley Common afforded sufficient space for large-scale military manoeuvres involving thousands of men in simulated set-piece engagements, sometimes, as above and below, witnessed by royal personages.*

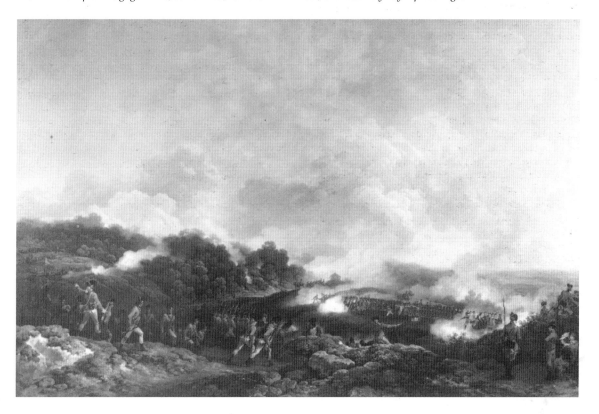

ON GUARD

The militia muster was again held at Warley in 1793 when the revolutionary regime in France once again threatened invasion. Lord Petre raised a substantial company of volunteers as further proof of his loyalty. In 1798 detailed contingency plans were drawn up for emergency transport arrangements and food supplies. Richard Williams was appointed as Brentwood's 'conductor', with a fleet of ten waggons under his command.

Around 1805 permanent barracks were finally built to house two thousand cavalry at Little Warley Common, less than a day's march from Tilbury, where troops could embark for foreign service. A decade later the inhabitants of Great Warley collected £25 12s 6d for the veterans of "the signal victory of Waterloo". Those veterans would have included men of the 44th Foot which was later to make its home at Warley. The regiment had previously distinguished itself at Salamanca in 1812 by capturing the eagle standard of the French 62nd regiment. The eagle was added to their regimental badge and when the barracks finally closed Barrack Road was renamed Eagle Way to commemorate the valour of the 44th.

After the ending of the Napoleonic wars in 1815 the barracks were intermittently occupied until they were bought by the East India Company in 1842 as a training centre for the contingent of a thousand replacement troops it raised and sent out each year. For many who never returned from that harsh posting recollections of beery evenings in a Brentwood tavern may well have represented a last fond memory of their native land.

The Company not only extended the barracks but also built forty cottages as married quarters and an imposing chapel, designed by Sir Matthew Wyatt, so that the 'riding house' would no longer have to double up as a place of worship. Ironically 'John Company' was soon to be wound up as a result of the 'Great Rebellion' of 1857 and control of Warley barracks passed to the War Office. Following Cardwell's army reforms of 1870 the former 44th and 56th regiments of the line, which had recruited in east and west Essex respectively, were amalgamated to become the first and second battalions of the Essex Regiment. This, together with the county's militia contingents, was to occupy Warley as its headquarters from 1873 until the evacuation and demolition of the barracks in 1959. Warley barracks has also at various times accommodated the Queen's Regiment, the Norfolk Regiment, the Middlesex Regiment and the Grenadier Guards.

64. Base camp of Empire – the East India Company barracks at Warley.

65. *Brentwood Drill Hall, Ongar Road, opened in 1886, served as the headquarters of the 4th Battalion, Essex Regiment.*

66. *The modern Essex Regiment chapel at Great Warley, originally built by the East India Company.*

Georgian Pastoral

Improved communications not only benefited through-travel and commerce but also enlarged the possibilities of a 'town-and-country' existence. The Rev. Philip Morant, author of a pioneering *History of Essex*, observed in 1768 that Brentwood "is at so small a distance from the capital, it affords an agreeable retirement to several citizens, upon which it is lately much improved in buildings." The *Chelmsford Chronicle* reiterated the point with specific reference to South Weald a generation later in 1796:

> "The situation, in many places, is inviting, as well for the healthiness of the soil, as for the conveniency of its distance from London and the richness of the prospects which in various places it affords. To this circumstance we may ascribe the settling of many wealthy persons ... Besides these there are many very good houses that cannot properly be called seats, but which are either the residence or retirement of families of good fortune ... ".

As a consequence gentry of purely local origin were outnumbered by incomers. The *Chelmsford Chronicle* specifically mentioned Thomas Tower of Weald Hall, a London lawyer, Sir Thomas Parker, Lord Chief Baron of the Exchequer and the Honourable Captain Hamilton. Anthony Collins of Bois Hall, Navestock was another London lawyer. Other recruits to the ranks of gentry came from a mercantile background as the would-be lessor of a Navestock residence was clearly aware, advertising its availability in a coffee-house in Exchange Alley.

The area also offered good recreation for the sportsman. Game books from South Weald for the year 1737 record not only pheasant and partridge but also quail and snipe and deer. There were occasional race meetings on Warley Common around the mid-century and others at Navestock. Navestock was also the home of local cricket, certainly by 1784, possibly before. In the 1790s the 'Essex Cricket Club' held fortnightly matches at the Green Man, Navestock Side. The membership included Lord Petre and Lord Winchilsea. Lord Petre also kept a pack of hounds in kennels at old Thorndon Hall.

Music was another source of distraction. In 1763 a Mr Arnold opened a Music Assembly Room at Great Warley with a "fine new organ" and the promise of mid-morning concerts by "some of the best performers from London". Tea, coffee, chocolate and wine were served to the audience and hay and stabling were included in the price of tickets.

Ladies kept boredom at bay by organising excursions and extended visits. Writing from

67. Navestock Hall, imposing home of the Waldegrave family.

Great Warley Place in June 1771 Mary Martin explained to her then fiancé Isaac Rebow of Wivenhoe Park "the reason it seems of our being so suddenly and pressingly invited was to ... have some little concerts". Mary and her sister played organ and harpsichord, their host, Captain Adams, the violin and other members of the company flutes and cello. Daytime diversions included "Trap Ball, Haymaking and Walking". Mary was still there ten days later "as Mrs Adams cannot live unless I favour her with my company". Further treats in prospect include a "little trip in the Brentwood machine" and "then all come up to London in the yatch" {sic} from Grays.

VANISHED GLORY

From a national, rather than a purely local, point of view the most eminent local family were the Waldegraves of Navestock. In 1686 the fourth baronet was created Baron Waldegrave. In 1729 his son was created Earl Waldegrave. He abandoned the old timber-framed Tudor manor house and built a fine brick mansion of nine bays, set off with formal gardens, an ornamental lake, a mile long double avenue of trees and an extensive deer park. This grandeur was to last less than a century. In 1811 the house was demolished and the materials sold off. Perhaps this drastic step was triggered by the death of the Hon. Edward Waldegrave, drowned off Falmouth on returning from the evacuation of Corunna in 1809. A flamboyant monument was commissioned from John Bacon the Younger of Southwark to stand in the parish church of St Thomas. It depicts "a mother weeping over the canteen of her son, which has been washed ashore, and in the background is seen a boy unfurling the British standard." Frances, Countess Waldegrave remained attached to the site of the former mansion and had a summer-house built there.

The Waldegraves had acquired the former property of St Paul's from Queen Mary Tudor and went on adding to it, acquiring the manors of Slades, Bois Hall and Loft Hall. In 1770 John, third Earl Waldegrave organised the enclosure of the former common, bagging 350 of its 502 acres for himself. By 1840 the family owned some 3,000 acres, almost three-quarters of the entire parish.

68. The Waldegrave mausoleum, Navestock, scheduled for removal in 2002.

69. Alexander Pope (1688-1744).

70. Kelvedon Hall, the seat of John Wright.

STATEMENTS OF TASTE

The combination of wealth and leisure conjured the threat of ennui. Foreign travel was one remedy. Hugh Smith of South Weald undertook the Grand Tour; his portrait, painted by Pompeo Batoni in Rome, can be seen in Spencer House in St James's. The seventh Lord Petre was said to spend six hours a day dressing his hair, although it was his prank of cutting a lock of Arabella Fermor's hair, rather than his eccentric devotion to his own coiffure, which inspired Alexander Pope to write *The Rape of the Lock* in 1712. The poet hoped that his satire would reconcile the Petres and Fermors who had become seriously estranged by the incident but his efforts proved in vain. Petre married a rich Lancashire heiress but died shortly afterwards of smallpox.

The most common gentlemanly diversion, of course, was building and landscaping the family seat or upgrading the local church. Numerous examples of 'improvement' can be seen from the late seventeenth century onwards. Bois Hall at Kelvedon Hatch dates from 1687. Shenfield Place was built *c.*1689 to the designs of the versatile scientist Robert Hooke. Jewells (now the Tower Arms) at South Weald dates from 1704. The plan of Blackmore House, with its four square angle towers, was emphatically un-Georgian but its windows and facing bricks date it – or its refacing – to *c.* 1715-20. In 1718 Ralph Bridges spent £800

71. The Pool Garden at Kelvedon Hall.

72. Boyles Court.

on a new vicarage and gardens at South Weald. In the same year a new west tower was added to St Peter's at Little Warley. Kelvedon Hall has rainwater heads dated 1725 and 1740 and had its own Oratory. Nearby Brizes dates from *c.* 1720 and featured a spectacularly grand staircase. The Hyde at Fryerning of 1719 was similarly dramatised in 1761 when (Sir) William Chambers, then the rising star of the architectural profession, was called in to transform five rooms into an imposing entrance hall. After much of the Tudor fabric of Hutton Hall was destroyed by fire, it was rebuilt from 1720 onwards. At South Weald, Gilstead Hall (formerly Wealdside) dates from 1726, Ditchleys from 1729. Hugh Smith, lord of the manor of South Weald from 1732 to 1745, landscaped its park. In 1753 the church of St Nicholas was rebuilt at Kelvedon Hatch to replace its decayed medieval predecessor. Sir John Tyrrell, who died in 1766, was commemorated with a monument by the prolific and highly talented J T Nollekens. In 1776 Boyles Court was rebuilt at Great Warley for the Lescher family to the designs of Thomas Leverton, the distinguished architect of Bedford Square, Bloomsbury. In 1778

Robert Adam was called in to Weald Hall to create a new dining-room and reface the south front. In 1788 the gardens at Brizes, Kelvedon Hatch, were re-planned by landscape architect Richard Woods, who settled in Ingrave in 1783 and became Lord Petre's surveyor.

Overshadowing all of these projects, however, was the building programme of the Petre family. In 1735 Robert James, eighth Lord Petre (1713-42), built St. Nicholas' church at Ingrave *(ill. 74)*. Professor Pevsner compliments it as "the most remarkable eighteenth century church in the county " and likens it to the work of Hawksmoor, though the architect is unknown. Petre also commissioned the distinguished Venetian master Giacomo Leoni (1686-1746) to remodel Thorndon Hall in a Palladian mode which included a majestic Corinthian portico of six columns.

The eighth Lord deserves, however, to be remembered primarily as a horticulturalist and landscape designer. St Nicholas, it must be admitted, was built to replace the former parish church, demolished to make way for the laying out of a gigantic lawn. Petre took over responsibility for the gardens at Thorndon when he was only sixteen and was elected a Fellow of the Royal Society at eighteen. He pioneered the use of hothouses or 'stoves', rivalled only by those at Oxford and Chelsea, to produce exotics such as pineapples and to achieve the first successful propagation of a camellia in England in 1740. In 1733 he had elaborate plans for a major re-design

73. *Hutton Hall., c1750, the seat of Daniel Booth.*

of the gardens drawn up by the French surveyor Bourginion. It featured a grand axis in the manner of Le Notre but offset this with a myriad of 'localities' and long screens and clumps of trees, twenty thousand of European species and ten thousand from Asia and America. A friend of the distinguished botanist Peter Collinson, who hailed him as "the ornament and delight of the age he lived in", Petre proved especially skilled in selecting trees and shrubs to make striking contrasts of form, colour and texture, "painting with living pencils" as Collinson called it. He also successfully transplanted two dozen fully-grown elms, sixty feet in height. The humble mill-pond was re-shaped as a formal lake and a mount raised for a dovehouse, to the west of the house, as well as two more at the northern end of the main avenue, planted with larch and evergreens and topped with cedars of Lebanon. Petre was doomed to an early grave which left his great scheme uncompleted and the estate bequeathed to a new-born infant. Collinson supervised the dispersal of the contents of his nursery to other great estates only too pleased to receive its treasures but when he revisited Thorndon twenty years later was dispirited to see the nursery overgrown, the 'stoves' empty of plants and the house sadly dilapidated.

74. *St Nicholas church, Ingrave, a bold composition by an unknown architect.*

D O M.
ET DIVO NICOLAO SACRVM
ROBERTVS IACOBVS PETRE BARO DE WRITTLE
AMBABVS AEDIBVS ET PAROECIIS
THORNDON OCCIDENTALI ET INGRAVE
IN VNAM EX S C COALESCENTIBVS
POSVIT MDCCXXXIV

75. *Noblesse oblige – the prominent plaque above the entrance to St Nicholas, Ingrave records the generosity of its builder, Lord Petre.*

76. *Fitzwalters at Shenfield c.1800, the seat of Thomas Wright Esq., featuring an elegant bridge, hexagonal lodge and boundary fence.*

77 and 78. Two views of Thorndon Hall. The magnificent architecture and extensive grounds made it a favourite subject for artists and engravers.

From 1764 onwards an entirely new Thorndon Hall was built a mile to the north of the original, at the head of his father's grand axis, for Robert Edward, the ninth Baron Petre (1742-1801), who had now come of age. The architect was Chambers' great rival, James Paine (1725-89), working on a scale of grandeur which eclipsed all other residences of the locality. The rectangular central block of the new house was eleven bays wide, fronted by Leoni's recycled portico and connected either side by nine-bay colonnades to three-bay pavilions. In the east wing was a chapel rising through two storeys. Paine also built a picturesque farmhouse on a nearby hill to complement the grounds, which were laid out between 1766 and 1772 by Capability Brown at a cost of £5000. Brown, characteristically, 'deformalised' the lake but left the Octagon Plantation unmolested.

LOCAL LEADERSHIP

The occupants of the grander houses varied in their relationship to the surrounding community. From 1723 until 1749 the Moat House at Brook Street was the country home of William Wheatley, a London commodity broker who took little part in local affairs and relied on a manager to run the farming side of his property. His successor, Thomas Wybert, a local carpenter who had prospered to become a builder and landlord, was an activist, serving as Churchwarden and Overseer of the Poor. In 1762 the property was taken over by another Londoner, Nathaniel Neal, a partner in the optimistically named Million Bank. He died within a year but his widow lived on there until her death in 1785.

Hugh Smith of Weald Hall attended vestry meetings frequently and sent a proxy when he could not. By contrast, Thomas Tower, the successful London lawyer who bought Weald Hall in 1752, was an unashamed week-ender, driving down from town on a Saturday and returning the following Monday or Tuesday. He did, to be fair, rebuild three local almshouses in the 1770s. Thomas Brand-Hollis of The Hyde, Fryerning (*see p.112*) served not once but twice in a ten year period as overseer of the poor and even Earl StVincent (*see p.115*) did his turn as surveyor of local highways. At Stondon Massey William Taylor-How left a legacy for the village schoolmaster and P H Meyer supported the village school financially and led the local Volunteers.

79. The Belvedere at Weald Hall, an eighteenth-century embellishment.

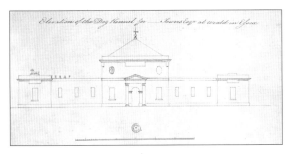

80. Even the dog kennels at Weald Hall were conceived on a majestic scale.

At Great Warley the eminent Huguenot surveyor Peter Bernard Scale (1739-1826) became a founding committee member of a local association for prosecuting felons.

There was more to local community service than a willingness to devote time to administrative chores and support local good causes. Occasionally office-holding carried real risks. Mary Martin, staying with the Adams family at Great Warley Place in the spring of 1772, reported that a large but peaceable crowd assembled there to ask the master, in his capacity as a magistrate, what would be done about sky-high food prices. He "assured them he would have the peace kept ... but they preferred breaking the peace and so went and attempted to regulate Brentwood Market (i.e. enforce sales at pre-shortage prices), for which they got heavily punished by the townspeople and his Worship's warrants have gone forth."

SELF-MADE MAN

Most of the locality's gentry had either inherited their fortune or made it in London. Daniel Sutton (1735-1819) of Ingatestone accumulated his by a combination of hard graft and a buccaneering flair for marketing his medical services. He was born the second son of a Suffolk surgeon and apothecary, Robert Sutton (?1708-88). When the elder Sutton's first born son, also named Robert, nearly died after being carelessly inoculated against smallpox by a professional colleague, Sutton senior devoted himself to studying and improving the process. Robert Sutton learned that by taking his lymph matter from immature pustules he could greatly diminish both the risk of transmitting a virulent infection and the degree of disfigurement caused by the procedure. He also determined to maintain closer control of his patients by establishing inoculation houses

where they could receive up to a month's nursing after-care. Their confinement also curtailed the risk that they might infect others in the early stages of their recovery. The first inoculation house opened in 1757 and by 1758, so great was the demand, that four were in operation. By 1760 Sutton senior had agents in sixteen locations, stretching from south Norfolk to north-east Essex. It was at this point that Daniel Sutton, initially his father's pupil, returned from a period of further instruction with an Essex physician to join his father and brother Robert in the still expanding family business. In 1762 Robert was put in charge of a further two inoculation houses. Daniel, doubtless resentful, and scenting better prospects closer to London, decided to branch out on his own and set up at Mill Green, Fryerning in 1763. The location was near, but not on, a major highway, within reach of the capital – but beyond the jurisdictional limits of the College of Physicians.

Earning a fabulous two thousand guineas in his very first year of independent practice must have convinced Daniel Sutton that he had made the right move. Local critics of his business were silenced by his offer to inoculate the poor for free. Henceforth, propelled by ferocious ambition, not to mention avarice, Sutton completely overshadowed his father and brother by operating on a Herculean scale. In 1765 he inoculated 923 subjects in the first twenty weeks of the year. He now had three inoculation houses at Ingatestone, where clients paid three, four or six guineas for their treatment. That year his practice grossed £6,500. The following year he single-handedly curbed an embryonic epidemic at Maldon, inoculating 487 in just one day. He could well afford the residence known as the Maisonette, set in thirty-nine acres of grounds, which he bought at Fryerning that same year. At the Summer Assizes in Chelmsford, however, he was charged with starting an epidemic in the county town. As the local Chelmsford practitioners all practised inoculation Sutton could successfully plead that the case was unprovable and motivated by professional malice. As though making a spectacular and sustained gesture of defiance to his antagonists in the course of 1766 Sutton inoculated 7,816 subjects. This brought his grand total since 1763 to 13,792, plus another six thousand inoculated by his assistants.

In 1767 Sutton affirmed his gentry status by obtaining a grant of arms and adopting the motto 'Safely, Quickly and Pleasantly'. By then his business empire embraced 47 franchised partnerships, stretching into Wales, Ireland, the Netherlands, France, Jamaica and Virginia. Sutton's career reached its zenith at that point. He was shortly to be eclipsed in popular estimation by a rival, Thomas Dimsdale, and subsequently undermined as the generality of medical practitioners began to master the procedure. In the 1790s Jenner's superior technique, vaccination, rendered Sutton's methods entirely obsolete. Sutton lived on for another quarter of a century, embittered and forgotten, to die in his Bloomsbury residence.

WORKING LIVES

Proximity to London may have meant persons of means and leisure in the Brentwood locality were more numerous than was the general rule, as contemporaries were wont to remark, but the vast majority of the population still had to labour for a living. Farm work was still the largest employer. Essex was progressive and expansive in its attitudes, as the government's official agriculturalist Arthur Young readily attested in the 1790s, singling out Earl St Vincent for particular praise:

> " what a spectacle to see this gallant veteran, after carrying the glory of the national flag to so high a pitch, sit down in health and spirits to the amusements of agriculture and entering with vigour and intelligence into the minutiae of the art".

Despite receiving the fabulous sum of £3000 a year as a pension, the admiral apparently rose at four every morning to supervise work on his estate.

The Norfolk system of crop rotation was taken up in Ingatestone, where the root crops were used for fodder and systematic manuring was also undertaken. Lord Petre bought threshing machines from Norwich. Around Fryerning Wadham College encouraged its tenants to 'stub up' woodland and turn it over to arable. This would have provided welcome employment for the village, whose population expanded from 450 in 1778 to 646 by 1801. At Buttsbury woods were

converted to pasture and much of Navestock Heath was also enclosed. Dairying was important at Navestock and Kelvedon Hatch.

The presence of substantial gentry households in the neighbourhood created a demand not only for domestic servants but also for the services of local craftsmen to keep the essential markers of status – buildings, carriages and clothes – in good repair. In 1794 Ingatestone is known to have had a bricklayer, a glazier and two carpenters, a saddler, a wheelwright and a coachmaker and five tailors and two shoemakers. The manufacture of bricks and tiles created other non-farming jobs at Blackmore and Brentwood. Brentwood also still had a few weavers and tanners and, unusually, there was also a rural tannery at Little Warley. An Ingatestone brewery, large enough to supply twelve inns, created further employment, not only in brewing but in the daily task of distribution. Passing traffic boosted retailing. Records of the Inspectors of Weights reveal that in the period 1770-74 Brentwood had fifteen shops, four bakers and three butchers, Ingatestone and Fryerning six shops, three bakers and two butchers. Ingrave got a shop of its own a decade later.

One particular skilled trade that was well represented locally was that of land surveyor, though usually this was a part time occupation, combined with some other business. John Dew of Brentwood was an auctioneer and bookseller and stationer. Philip Whittington of Brentwood was an estate bailiff for Lord Petre. Harvey of Kelvedon was an auctioneer and estate bailiff. Dayles of Buttsbury and George Hutson of Hutton were both farmers. George Sangster of Brentwood was an auctioneer (of wine as well as land) and nurseryman, with a substantial seven-acre establishment at Brook Street, where he also sold ornamental deer. In 1794 Joseph Golding took over both of Sangster's businesses but was gone by 1798. Fitchatt, Taylor and de Freis of Brentwood were all teachers. Fitchatt, not a university man, nevertheless owned his own school and prospered sufficiently to send his son to Cambridge and to buy land in Brentwood and Horndon. Fitchatt junior seems not to have enjoyed this not inconsiderable inheritance because he "had to go abroad" and in 1774 left for Barbados.

Railway Revolution

AGE OF IMPROVEMENT

By 1788 Brentwood's High Street was built up almost continuously but the built-up area expanded little over the succeeding half century. The period of the French wars was one of stagnation. The two annual fairs still attracted cattle dealers from as far away as Scotland and Wales but the weekly market which had been held since the town's foundation fizzled out in the last decade of the eighteenth century. In 1803 the authors of *The Beauties of England and Wales* referred slightingly to Brentwood's buildings as "irregular and mean". The workhouse in Back Street had to be enlarged in 1805 and 1828 as the population more than doubled between the first census in 1801, when it stood at 1,007 and 1841, when it reached 2,362. South Weald also increased but less dramatically, from 881 to 1,450. Its pastoral air still inspired praise, as from Pigot's *Essex Trade Directory* for 1832-3:

"Nature has been liberal in dispensing her favours around here; and the residents have managed their operations with such taste as to produce one of the most beautiful and picturesque retreats in the county; the gardens, the extensive pleasure grounds and grand scenery, are objects which cannot fail to attract notice and give delight."

The same publication likewise praised Thorndon Hall as being

"in the best style of architecture and fitted up with superior elegance and taste, commanding prospects as rich and varied as can well be imagined", whereas Ingatestone Hall was dismissed as "an antique but irregular pile".

The increase in Brentwood's inhabitants was squeezed into the existing town, but an 'age of improvement' was clearly beginning. In 1828 a new weighbridge and toll gates were built at Shenfield. In 1833 James McAdam, son of the eminent Scottish engineer J L McAdam, supervised the upgrading of the Shenfield-Chelmsford Road, thus effecting "a great alteration and improvement". In the same year C T Tower of Weald Park convened a meeting of potential investors to consider the possibility of making the Mardyke navigable from Purfleet up to Childerditch, though the scheme was dropped a year later.

Pigot's *Directory* noted that Ingatestone "though once a market town, can now only be designated as a village", its population of 789 being seven less than that of Mountnessing. The author was even more dismissive of Hutton: "contains nothing worthy of observation." During the 1820s the populations of Little Warley, Ingrave and East Horndon all fell slightly, against the national trend of rapid expansion. In Great Warley it fell by almost a hundred, presumably because the barracks was temporarily unoccupied.

Coaching was still in its heyday, thanks largely to the improvements in road construction which McAdam himself had pioneered, and coaches were passing through Brentwood and Ingatestone quite literally almost every hour. The setting up of new milestones and cast iron finger posts implies the continuance of a brisk traffic of private travellers as well.

In 1835 a new St Thomas's church was built on what had been a nursery garden south of High Street some three hundred metres south-east of the medieval chapel. The chapel was now deemed too cramped for worship and converted for use as a National (i.e. Church of England) school until most of it was demolished *c.* 1869, a casualty of 'progress', having stood for six and a half centuries. Ironically, the new St Thomas's, designed by James Savage, an eminent architectural consultant and designer of the much admired St Luke's, Chelsea, proved to be so poorly built that the tower fell down and the whole structure had to be replaced in the 1880s. The curate at the time of the original translation from chapel to church was Francis Rhodes, father of Cecil Rhodes.

In 1837 St. Helen's chapel was consecrated to provide for Catholic worship.

AGE OF STEAM

After the collapse of a number of abortive schemes to drive a railway out from the capital into its Essex hinterland an Act of Parliament finally brought the Eastern Counties Railway company into existence in 1836. It would have its terminus in Shoreditch. Liverpool Street, the last of the major London termini, would not materialise until 1874. From Shoreditch the line would run via Romford, Brentwood and Chelmsford to Colchester and then eventually on to Norwich. The work of construction was entrusted to John Braithwaite and C B Vignoles. Braithwaite was an extremely versatile character, who had built the first locomotive to run a mile in under a minute, cast the Portland Place statue of Queen

81. *St Thomas's church, Brentwood; drawing by W.W. Brown. Though rebuilt by an eminent archiect in 1835, it was destined to last less than half a century.*

82. *Following the full restoration of civil rights to Catholics in 1829, there was a boom in building places of worship for them. St Helen's was an early example of the newly fashionable Gothic style.*

Victoria's father, the Duke of Kent, and invented a practicable steam-powered fire engine. In 1837 he founded the *Railway Times* newspaper.

In constructing the Eastern Counties line he would introduce from America an excavating machine and a steam-powered pile-driver. Vignoles can have had far less direct involvement in the project being simultaneously engaged on many others elsewhere, both in England and on the Continent. In 1841 University College, London appointed him to Britain's first ever professorship in civil engineering.

Construction of the line began in March 1837 and a first section, reaching as far as Romford, opened in June 1839 with a celebratory inaugural run for a company of invited guests which included the Persian ambassador: "The trains will start from the Temporary Station, Devonshire Street, Mile End, Turnpike Gate at one o'clock and proceed leisurely along the line to Romford, where after remaining an hour for the Company to partake of refreshments they will return to London." Two trains, with a band in the front carriage of each, steamed majestically abreast on the two tracks to pass through the intermediate stations at Stratford and Ilford and finally disgorge their passengers at Romford station, where luncheon awaited them in an adjoining field. The service thus inaugurated offered a choice of seven

trains per day each way, running between the civilized hours of 9am and 7pm.

The section connecting Brentwood to London via Romford opened on 1 July 1840 and initially offered a service of five trains a day. Before the year was out, however, the first fatalities occurred when a passenger train ran off the lines near Brook Street. In the same year the rector of Great Warley recorded the death of twenty-three-year-old Henry Jay, killed "by leaping out of a carriage on the railway after his hat had fallen off." By 1842 fifteen year old Elizabeth Fry – of the Quaker family of prison reformer Elizabeth Fry – was able to travel to the family's country home, Warley Lodge, by railway via Stratford from her home in Plaistow.

Extending the line beyond Brentwood meant passing through seven miles of property owned by Lord Petre, for which he claimed £20,000 in respect of the real value of the land and a whopping £100,000 in compensation, six times the sum originally offered. The ECR directors agreed but defaulted until Petre took them to Chancery and agreed to accept the money in payments staggered over five years.

Extending the line onwards from Brentwood also involved the challenging task of making a major cutting, crossed by the Seven Arches bridge, which incorporated bricks from the demolished

83. The Seven Arches Bridge and railway cutting – a major engineering challenge.

84. *Brentwood Station in Edwardian times – note the absence of motor vehicles.*

85. *Shenfield Station, early 20th century.*

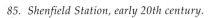

86. *The road to the City – Station Lane, Ingatestone.*

Mill Green House at Ingatestone. Geological complications ruined several contractors in the early stages but the work was concluded successfully and profitably by a local man, Thomas Hill. The spoil from the cutting, dumped in heaps, transformed the hitherto quite flat southern end to Shenfield Common. The inaugural run through the cutting turned into a disappointing fiasco when the engine failed just beyond the new station at Hutton and the trip had to be abandoned. Shortly afterwards several workmen were killed on a fatefully foggy day when they misjudged the direction of an approaching train and jumped into its path. In August 1840 a train passing through Brook Street too fast jumped the rails, causing numerous injuries among its twenty-four passengers.

By 1843 it was at last possible to reach Colchester and by 1846 Ipswich. By 1848 two stockbrokers, possibly Brentwood's first City commuters, are known to have been in residence. In the same year the station was described as "one of the handsomest ... on the Eastern Counties Railway." Noting the low level of empty houses in the county's most thriving towns in 1851, the author of *Essex and the Industrial Revolution* opines that Brentwood "seems to have been one of the first dormitory towns created by the railway." By 1854 West End theatres were advertising in ECR timetables in the hope of attracting audiences in to evening performances.

EXPANSION

When the railway station opened at Brentwood it encouraged the expansion of the town southwards. Unsurprisingly, brickfields were developed in the station area to meet local demand for construction. Queen's Road and New Road were laid out by 1844 and by 1848 a hundred new houses and a steam-powered corn mill had been built. Other steam mills were to be built at Ingatestone and Navestock. In 1863 Fielder's brewery was established.

The Brentwood Hall estate was sold off for development in 1842 by the Kavanagh family. It covered almost two hundred acres and over half was bought for the projected Essex Lunatic Asylum. Together with the opening of the barracks at Warley in 1843 and of the Shoreditch Agricultural and Industrial School on London Road, built a decade later to accommodate three hundred workhouse children, this stimulated development to the south of the railway line. A new parish, Christ Church, Warley, was accordingly created in 1855. In the same year William Burgess and Sir Kingsmill Grove Key opened their agricultural engineering works in Queen's Road. Their enterprise was directly inspired by the Great Exhibition of 1851 at which the McCormick mechanical reaper from the USA had been regarded by *The Times* as such a revelation as in itself to justify the entire exhibition. Unlike most comparable devices it was both efficient and robust. Burgess and Key were appointed English agents with licence to produce an adapted version of the machine, better suited to the heavier English crops. Although their model was soon superseded by rivals they diversified into new lines based on other American innovations, including a winnowing machine and a liquid manure pump. By 1863 the firm had become a major source of local employment, with a labour force of 180. When it relocated to larger premises – the Victoria Works – on the Ongar Road in 1866 this led to more general expansion of Brentwood northwards.

Interestingly, the physical expansion of the town was accompanied by a degree of decongestion as the population had dipped slightly by 1851 to 2,205. South Weald also experienced a similar minor contraction to 1,383. In fact this can be explained by the fact that the 1841 figure had been temporarily boosted by the presence of construction crews working on the railway. In that year there were eighty labourers and their families at Mountnessing alone. The navvies were rough, tough and well-paid. Doubtless local inn-keepers liked their free-spending ways but the Chelmsford Petty Sessions Book of 1841 recorded that "In consequence of the outrageous behaviour of the Labourers employed on the Line of the Eastern Counties Railway at Margaretting, Mr Langly a respectable Inhabitant of that parish applied to the bench for the appointment of Special Constables for the preservation of the peace etc." In the same year labourers at Ingatestone complained to the same Sessions that their foreman had run off with the wages of ninety-three men. There was at least one positive outcome from the passage of the navvies. Thomas Wilcox, a Wesleyan navvy from Lincolnshire, established a Methodist chapel on Primrose Hill.

BRENTWOOD'S BOURGEOISIE

By mid-century Brentwood was already acquiring a strongly commercial character. Eight residents styled themselves 'gentleman' and there was also a naval captain in residence but they were greatly outnumbered by an elite of professionals including eleven insurance agents, nine teachers, half a dozen clergymen, four each of medical men and attorneys, three auctioneers, an actuary and a vet. There was also an artist/engraver and a drawing master. Modern bureaucracy was represented by a police superintendent, a 'gas manager' and the station-master and his two clerks, traditional bureaucracy by an assistant overseer of the poor, a church clerk and a sexton. Commercial occupations, however, were far more numerous. The food and drink trades employed thirteen bakers, eleven grocers, eleven inn-keepers and eight keepers of beer houses and six butchers, two fishmongers, a wholesale grocers, a greengrocer, a cow-keeper, a dealer in fish and game, an 'eating house' and a wine and porter merchant. Clothing the local inhabitants gave work to a dozen boot and shoe makers, ten milliners and dressmakers, eight tailors, two glovers, a staymaker, two clothiers and hatters and a clothes dealer. Other retailers included five drapers, four toyshops, four confectioners, three dealers in glass and china, three unspecified 'shopkeepers', two chemists, two ironmongers and a dealer in marine stores. There were also three bookseller/printers, one of whom also functioned as an auctioneer while the other doubled as the town's post office manager. The strongly agricultural nature of the town's hinterland is attested by the presence of three corn

dealers (two of whom were also coal merchants), three corn millers, two horse dealers, three each of saddlers, blacksmiths and wheelwrights, two nurserymen/seedsmen, a brewer and maltster, a pig dealer and currier and a leather cutter. The building trades were represented by five carpenters, four painters and plumbers and two bricklayers. Other local craftsmen included three watchmakers, two coopers, a monumental mason, a coach builder, a basket maker and a bird stuffer. The few service providers included a chimney-sweep and a hairdresser. By contrast Ingatesone had less than a dozen shops, half a dozen craftsmen, four inns and three beer-houses and South Weald's entire complement of tradesmen and craftsmen numbered less than twenty, including two millers, a gardener, a gamekeeper and the butler at Weald Hall. When Canon Last badgered the 12th Lord Petre to build a new Catholic church for Ingatestone, he refused outright: "I cannot consent so to cripple myself for a poor decaying town like Ingatestone".

PILLAR OF THE ESTABLISHMENT

Dr Cornelius Butler (1789-1871), son of an Ingatestone surgeon, settled in Brentwood in 1812. At that time the town had two other doctors. The vestry invited all three 'medical gentlemen' to tender for the care of the local poor on a three year contract on the understanding that the lowest offer would be accepted. Butler was appointed at a salary of nine pounds a year. Over the following half century he established himself as a virtual civic icon. A photograph taken near the end of his life shows a stout John Bull figure mounted on a white cob, which he rode to do his country rounds. Butler served as a governor of Brentwood School and also acted as the local registrar of births, deaths and marriages, signing the decennial census returns. He also made his own personal contribution to the local population, having two sons and nine daughters. Butler's eldest daughter married his assistant, John Bean, and accompanied him to India, where he became Surgeon Major to the East India Company. Their son, Edwin Bean, would become headmaster of Brentwood School. Butler also had a literary side and in 1848 published *Ingrebourne: or some account of Brentwood and its neighbourhood. Ingrebourne and other poems* appeared in 1884, after his death.

87. Brentwood High Street, c.1906, showing the Town Hall of 1864 on the right.

88. South Weald almshouses, rebuilt in the mid-nineteenth century in a mannered Gothic. Private charitable provision remained significant.

89. *The Petre almshouses at Ingatestone, an example of the 'model dwellings' beloved of contemporary architects.*

THE SHAPE OF THINGS TO COME

Modernity in the shape of artificial street-lighting came little more than a decade after it had begun to transform the capital itself. The Brentwood Gas Light and Coke Co. established itself in Crown Street in 1836 and in 1841 Brentwood voted to adopt gas-lighting generally. Another portent of modern urbanism was the opening of Brentwood's first police station in Coptfold Road in 1851. A County Court to complement it was built in New Road in 1848. Brentwood lagged, however, in respect of sanitation. There was an outbreak of smallpox in 1854. A Board of Health enquiry of 1857 was severely critical of the town's paving, water supply and drainage: "the general class of diseases prevailing here are of an inflammatory cast. Last year there was a good deal of fever but the mortality was not high. In 1854 smallpox was very prevalent. Absolute cholera was only fatal in one case ... the poorer class of dwellings are in a very bad state and overcrowding is common". Another enquiry a decade later was simi-

larly condemnatory. Indeed, the situation was so alarming that central government felt compelled to intervene and oblige the vestry to act – one of only seven instances in the entire country where it felt compelled to take this action. A piped water supply was laid on by the South Essex Waterworks Company in 1866. Brentwood's relatively high elevation in south Essex was to necessitate the construction of a reservoir at Herongate and a lifting station at Warley.

Emergent civic pride found expression in the erection of a monumental obelisk to honour the memory of Protestant martyr William Hunter in 1861. The decayed Assize House was pulled down in 1864 and in the same year a new Brentwood Town Hall was opened. Most of St Thomas's chapel was pulled down after 1869 when it was no longer considered fit to be used as a school. In 1873 Brentwood was finally established as a parish in its own right. In 1876 it was complimented as having "a clean, quiet, well-to-do and rather more 'genteel' look than is common in Essex towns. The suburbs are pretty and pleasant." The author was evidently unaware that during the 1874 election supporters of the rival Liberal and Conservative candidates rioted in the High Street. The Liberals had hired a German band to march at the head of their procession. When this was attacked by a Conservative mob the musicians took to their heels, abandoning their instruments. 1876 was also the year in which Essex County Cricket Club opted to base itself in Shenfield Road, though it moved on to Leyton a decade later. (The club did return to play several important matches at 'The Old County Ground' in the 1930s.) The last old-style Brentwood Fair was held in 1877, terminating a traditional institution in its six hundred and fiftieth year. Its passing symbolized the fact that the gains of the previous half century in terms of the comforts and conveniences of life were accompanied by losses, some less inevitable than others. In 1878 Thorndon Hall was severely damaged by fire.

Contemporaries were also aware of other losses. The Essex historian D W Coller noted in 1861 that Ingatestone's once thriving Wednesday cattle market had disappeared:

"Its market square ... has long been deserted by the dealer... Its inns ... have dwindled away beneath the pressure of the rail, which runs close to the town; and the once great thoroughfare whose trade drew sustenance from the stream of passing travellers, is now a quiet rural village."

Brentwood by contrast was characterised as

"one of the few places which have drawn new life and vigour from the railway ... The old houses have been much improved; new villas have sprung up around; almshouses, industrial schools and asylums of city companies have been built in the vicinity; and the town bears about it the appearance of prosperity and the signs of further extension."

RURAL IDYLL

Coller described the area around Brentwood approvingly as "thickly studded with mansions and parks, abounding as it does with scenes of rich rural beauty, and combining easy access to the business haunts and fashionable and political activity of the metropolis, with all the quiet enjoyments of thorough country life...".

In 1842 Warley Lodge was occupied by the Fry family. Fifteen-year-old Elizabeth was the granddaughter of prison reformer Elizabeth Fry, Britain's most famous Quaker, but her father was an Anglican and a JP and, though born a Friend, she would be christened at sixteen. Elizabeth's diary records that they returned from an extended New Year stay with "dearest grandmama" at Upton by means of the new 'railroad'. The Frys' amuse-

ments included drawing and walking, carriage drives into Brentwood, horseback rides over to Hutton and Shenfield, taking tea at the home of Lady English, evening readings of Shakespeare, cards, chess, draughts and "charades, games, dancing and singing" with neighbours. In July the ladies of the family drove over to Herongate to see their local team play a Brentwood side at cricket: "It is very interesting and amusing to watch this game when one has seen it all; to drop in in the middle is remarkably dull".

Elizabeth's diary reveals clearly, however, that she was serious, studious, attentive to sermons and even "enjoyed Milner's Church History", though she found *Don Quixote*" in most parts very tedious, although extremely clever". Glad to accompany "Mama to Childerditch to visit a poor woman", she also manned a stall at a great charity bazaar in the Mansion House: "We all returned home ... thoroughly knocked up ... heartily delighted to leave the bustle, dirt and din of London."

While Brentwood developed fitfully towards full-fledged urbanism South Weald maintained an almost tangible aura of rurality. Not until 1848 did it even acquire a post office. At Brook Street the visitor could see a smithy and a water-mill in operation. South Weald's manorial court was still regularly convened. Christopher Tower,

90. *Weald Hall, c.1830. Its grounds were greatly extended in the early nineteenth century. Prize livestock completed the perfection of the scene.*

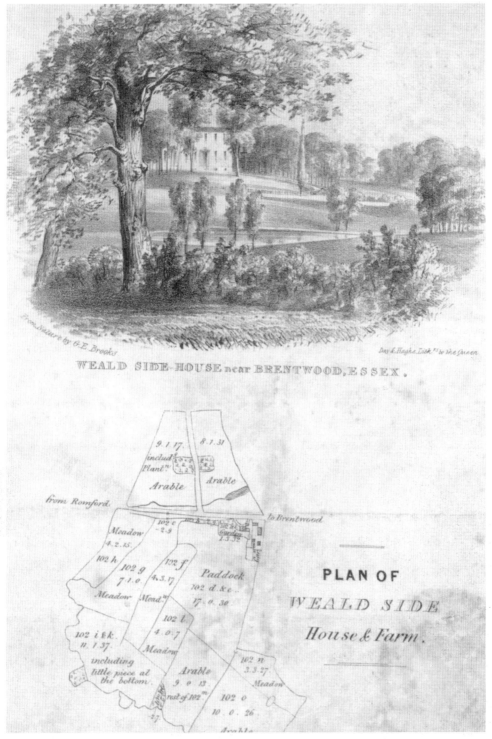

91. Wealdside House and Farm, 'drawn from nature' by G.E. Brooks. The house was later used for a boys' academy.

squire for more than half a century (1810-67), vigorously utilised an Inclosure Act of 1812 to enclose much traditional waste, doubling the size of his estate. He also restored the great hall at Weald Hall and stocked his park with a flock of Cashmere goats. While Squire Tower took advantage of his fortune and longevity to aggrandise his demesne, South Weald's vicar, Charles Belli, utilised his wealth and long tenure of office (1823-76) to undertake good works, starting with making himself more comfortable. Shunning the existing vicarage, dating from 1718, in 1825 he had a new one built to the west of it in Vicarage (now Wigley Bush) Lane to the designs of Henry Hakewill, the architect of Rugby school, who also had a profitable sideline in designing gentlemen's country residences. The project was still not quite finished seven years later and had run up costs of £6,650, of which £5,720 had come from Belli's own pocket. Even he conceded that this was "a fearful result". Considering that even Jane Austen would have reckoned such a sum a marriageable fortune it certainly was. But Belli evidently had plenty left. He put £20,000 towards the building of the church at Bentley and also contributed to the building of new schools in Bentley and Crescent Road and to the reconstruction of St Thomas's in Brentwood. In 1868 South Weald church was extensively restored at Belli's expense under the direction of the notable, if often heavy-handed, S S Teulon. His reconstruction was radical. The medieval north aisle was demolished and replaced with a new nave, chancel and organ chamber, while the old nave and chancel became the south aisle and chapel. The whole building was also re-roofed and a south porch added and the top stage of the Tudor tower rebuilt. Most of the old furnishings, including a west gallery, three-decker pulpit and pews made from the recycled medieval rood screen, were swept away. The altar tomb of Sir Anthony Browne was also destroyed.

The rural character of South Weald recommended it as a residential area for the wealthy. One distinctive sub-community consisted of Roman Catholics. A wealthy Portuguese priest, Emanuel Dias Santos, occupied Pilgrims Hall on

92. *St Paul's church, Bentley, built largely through the generosity of South Weald's vicar, Charles Belli.*

Ongar Road from 1814 until his death in 1834. The house later became a boarding school, whose pupils included the enterprising Mr Beeton, whose future wife would write the classic *Book of Household Management*. Wealdside, long the home of the Catholic Wrights, also became a school. Other Romish residents included the Leschers, who occupied the manor of Boyles and the Honourable Frederick Petre. The Leschers, a mercantile family from Alsace, arrived in England around 1778 and married into the Walmesleys, a Catholic family long established in South Weald, but ultimately of Lancashire stock. There were also several prominent representatives of what came to be humorously known as the 'beerage'. Luptons in Wigley Bush Lane was the home of Edward Ind, partner in the major Romford brewery. Another partner, Octavius Coope MP, lived at Rochetts, former home of Earl St Vincent. Osgood Hanbury lived at Hou Hatch, Weald Road. Less exalted residents could be found out along the Ongar Road at the spot known as Gallows Corner where the 1871 census revealed it to be a permanent encampment of gypsies, basket-makers and sundry hawkers, living in vans and tents. If they symbolised a fading rural past, the arrival of the telegraph in 1872 stood for the future.

Victorian Villages

William White's *History, Gazetteer and Directory of the County of Essex*, first published in 1848, not only offers much basic information about the villages around Brentwood but, through its criteria for the selection and arrangement of that information, an insight into contemporary social values. The attention paid to churches, manor houses and lineages was far greater than any concern with recent change or future possibilities, though it does credit to White's researchers that they knew that "a large County Lunatic Asylum" was about to be built at Warley. Its foundation stone was laid in 1851 and the first patients admitted in 1853. By 1860 there were 175 male and 251 female inmates. The regime was enlightened, with opportunities for farm and garden work, country walks and a ball at New Year.

While the villages treated in this chapter are all now in Brentwood's local government jurisdiction, in the mid-nineteenth century only half of them looked to Brentwood as their nearest urban centre. The clearest indicator of this is the source of the daily post. Letters for Blackmore, Doddinghurst and Mountnessing came from Ingatestone. Letters for East and West Horndon, Hutton, Ingrave and the Warleys came from Brentwood. Letters for Kelvedon Hatch and Stondon Massey came via Ongar and for Navestock via Romford.

SETTINGS AND SIZE

Each of White's entries begins with a general comment on the physical nature and aspect of each settlement. Blackmore was judged to be "a pleasant village, though in a low situation", Doddinghurst "pleasant but straggling" with "a fruitful loam ... pleasantly undulated", and Kelvedon Hatch a "scattered village, mostly on a green or common". The "long scattered village" of Great Warley, despite "heavy soil on a clay bottom" was still "fertile and well cultivated". Ingrave was singled out for special praise as "handsome ... delightfully situated". Shenfield, "neat and pleasant" was characterised as already a *de facto* suburb of Brentwood. At "fertile and picturesque" East Horndon and Herongate the "many neat houses" contrasted with the parsonage "a small mean building ... occupied by cottagers."

93. *Essex County Lunatic Asylum, one of a new generation of mental institutions created to share the burden previously borne by London's Bethlem Hospital.*

94. Salmons Farm at Ingrave.

95. The Foresters' Inn at Shenfield, c.1906

96. *The handsomely rebuilt Horse and Groom was doubtless sustained by the custom of nearby Warley Barracks. Notice the substantial delivery of beer awaiting transfer to the cellar.*

97. *The Green at Great Warley, c.1906.*

98. *The Thatchers' Arms at Great Warley in the early 20th century – a view that has changed little.*

99. *The Headley Arms at Great Warley, c.1906, also doubtless a beneficiary of the custom of the barracks.*

Next came a note of the size of each community in terms of area and population. The largest, with seven hundred to a thousand inhabitants, were, in ascending order, Blackmore, Navestock, Mountnessing and Shenfield. In the medium rank with four to six hundred souls came Doddinghurst, Hutton, Kelvedon Hatch, East Hordon with Herongate and Ingrave. Little Warley, Childerditch and Stondon Massey each had less than three hundred residents.

RELIGION AND RANK

The contemporary importance of the religious establishment is attested by the inclusion of a concise description of each parish church and of any outstanding monuments, most notably the dramatic Waldegrave memorials in St Thomas's at Navestock. The names and status of individual clergy are recorded. So is the value of each living and the extent of any glebe land attached to it. The right of presentment was also noted. Often this was in local hands but at Navestock the advowson belonged to Trinity College, Cambridge and at Hutton to the Dean and Chapter of St Paul's. Finally it was recorded whether or not the tithes have been commuted for a cash payment. In Blackmore this had happened only a year previously, yielding a handsome £561 a year. Blackmore was also unusual in having its own Nonconformist place of worship, a Baptist chapel erected in 1841.

In an age which was supposed to represent the triumph of the bourgeoisie it is significant to note that the notion of 'the lord of the manor' was still taken very seriously and the descent of each manor, from Domesday through the Reformation redistributions and down to the present, was recorded at length. Lord Petre was naturally pre-eminent, being lord of the manor in Ingrave, Childerditch, Mountnessing and East and West Hordon. Lord Headley was lord of the manor in Great and Little Warley, the Countess of Waldegrave at Navestock and Earl de Grey at Shenfield. The 'lords' of the other manors were not titled but lordship usually implied ownership of most of the land – Lord Petre owned all of West Hordon and over 90% of Childerditch – but it did not necessarily imply more than occasional residence. The lord of the manor of Hutton was R Scholey Esq. who was also "owner of a great part of the soil" but "the Hall, a commodious but singular mansion in the Dutch style, was occupied by J A Macleod Esq.". Several villages were divided between two or more substantial own-

100. The architect's drawing of Grinstead Hall.

ers. In Blackmore the main landowners were Miss Crickitt of Smyth's Hall, Charles Vickerman of Blackmore House, three farmers and, interestingly, a bricklayer, Samuel Samuel. Doddinghurst was largely divided between Mr W Manbey of Doddinghurst Hall and Mr J Fane of Doddinghurst Place (*aka* Kensingtons). There were also corporate owners. The lordship of the manor of Fryerning was invested in Wadham College, Oxford. The lord of the manor of Stondon Massey, P H Meyer, occupied Stondon Place but the Revd G G Stonestreet and Christ's College, Cambridge were also substantial landowners. St Thomas's Hospital owned part of Great Warley.

Apart from actual landowners other leading residents were recorded by name and title. The most numerous were naturally the local tenant farmers. Blackmore had a dozen, Doddinghurst fourteen and Great Warley fifteen. The farmers at Ingrave and East Horndon must have operated on a considerable scale as there were only three and five of them respectively and seven each at Hutton and Little Warley. At Childerditch the eight farmers were the only residents of note apart from the vicar and the village schoolmistress. At Mountnessing there were twenty farmers, half in residences grand or at least ancient enough to merit a name.

Farmers were grouped together as a category but their social superiors were noted individually. It may, of course, be unduly trusting to assume that White's informants were equally persistent and successful in gathering information. If their efforts are taken at face value then, considering its size, Blackmore had few occu-

101. *Little Warley Hall, drawn by W. Bartlett and published in 1833.*

102. *Hutton Hall, c.1900.*

pants of note. Two residents were styled as gentlemen and two more as ladies and there was also a surgeon. Doddinghurst had not even this number. East Horndon by contrast could boast Philip Button Esq., Hepworth Boughey Esq., Joseph Antonio Pizzi, Gent. and Sir John Lister Kaye, Bart. who also had a place in Yorkshire. At Great Warley lived General Pinson Bonham, the widowed Lady Agnes English (with whom the Frys took tea) and the Revd Hastings Robinson *(see p.109)* and his curate. At Little Warley the pre-eminent residents, apart from the curate, were three officers at Warley barracks. The manager of the barracks canteen, William Boyman, was also listed, despite, one would have thought, his more ambiguous social standing. At Hutton genteel society consisted of the Misses Barrett, "gentlewomen", Mrs Townsend, four gentlemen and John Knowles Nix, a "professor of music and dancing". The Rector J C Haden MA was also "priest in ordinary to her Majesty". Ingrave was home to both the Rector of West Hordon with Ingrave and Lord Petre's chaplain. The ranking residents of Shenfield were Col. Cooch at Shenfield Place and Joseph Tasker at Middleton Hall.

THE BUSINESS OF LIVING

Tradesmen and craftsmen were also listed and provide a rough indicator of the local purchasing power of each community. Blackmore had four each of bricklayers and carpenters, three each of shoemakers, shopkeepers and bakers, two pubs, a beer-seller, a blacksmith, a butcher, a tailor and a collar-maker. The August fair, once granted to Blackmore Priory, "now continues three days – two for cattle and the last for pleasure." East Horndon was predominantly geared to the needs of local agriculture, having a corn miller, two bakers, two grocers and a tailor, a carpenter, saddler, wheelwright, shoemaker and gardener. Tiny Childerditch at the other end of the scale had only a single shop, a smithy and a beer-house. Doddinghurst had the Swan pub and a beer-house but no other commercial amenities at all.

Apart from the common employments noted above there were a few unusual ones. Hutton had a specialist hay-dealer. Ingrave was home to a 'relieving officer', a solicitor and a post-master. Shenfield had by far the most varied occupational structure. There were thirteen farmers along with such ancillary agricultural occupations as two corn millers, two blacksmiths and a carpenter/wheelwright. There were also two shoemakers. The rising professional classes were repre-

sented by a surgeon, a veterinary surgeon and the local (i.e. Brentwood) station-master and, less certainly, by the proprietrices of three ladies' boarding schools. Less exalted occupations included pot and tile maker, bricklayer, beer seller, gardener, shopkeeper and dressmaker, plus a builder/upholsterer.

A few women, apart from village schoolmistresses, are identified as working on their own account. Elizabeth Scrivener served as the village carrier at Blackmore; a woman ran the Chequers in Hutton and another was a beer seller there. The publican of the Green Man at Ingrave was a woman, Eleanor Oliffe and Ann Boardman was a shopkeeper there. Herongate had a female baker. At Doddinghurst Sarah Littlechild was listed as a farmer in her own right, as was Ann Case at Kelvedon Hatch and Sarah Haywood at Great Warley. Mary Ann Moore was Shenfield's professional dressmaker.

103. The sale of Great Warley Hall in 1813.

104. The main street in Great Warley on the eve of the railway age.

In small communities it was not uncommon for individuals to combine two or even more occupations. At Great Warley William Eldred doubled as constable and blacksmith/wheelwright and the publican of the Headley Arms was also a builder. At Little Warley William Deeks doubled as blacksmith and parish clerk. At Navestock the schoolmaster was also the parish clerk and the baker was also a shopkeeper, as was Lucy Lash who ran the Plough. At Kelvedon Hatch Charlotte Gandy, publican of the Eagle, was also a miller and the village schoolmaster William Nutt, doubled as post-master. A Hutton farmer was also a maltster and timber merchant. Mountnessing's Samuel Spackman was a wheelwright, joiner and blacksmith.

CHARITY BEGINS AT...

Every entry for a community concluded with a detailed listing of parish charities and their varied sources of income – most commonly rents from fields or cottages but also the yield from cash deposits and government securities. At Blackmore the rent from the Bull inn, by Thomas Almond's bequest of 1728, went to provide coals for the poor and other rents were used to fund distributions of bread and cash. There was also a house

105. The coat-of-arms of J F Wright.

J. F. Wright Esqr.

and garden, left as long ago as 1580, "for the use of six resident paupers." Finally there was a half acre let out for ten shillings a year which went to pay for bell-ropes for the parish church. There was a similar arrangement at Stondon Massey. At Navestock rents from bequeathed properties amounted to almost fifty pounds a year, distributed in "shoes, jackets and fagots". At Hutton nine acres had been vested in trust for the benefit of the poor in 1575; eight acres were let out for eight pounds while the remaining acre had been left as woodland to supply the poor with winter fuel. At Mountnessing the rent of Pichion's farm supported the Free School with a surplus paid to the two schoolmistresses for teaching 'poor children'. Presumably these were from families so poor that they could not afford to send them to school during normal hours because they needed whatever pence the children could earn from bird-scaring or clearing fields of stones. At Kelvedon Hatch the charitable effort was primarily a contemporary one where lord of the manor J F Wright of Kelvedon Hall, supported by the Misses Dolby of Brizes, was wont to "usually gladden the hearts of the poor parishioners with large distributions of beef, clothing etc. at Christmas."

CHANGE IN THE VILLAGE

Even a cursory glance through the census returns of a single village can illuminate both the outlines of its social structure and the broad changes affecting its daily life over decades. Detailed figures survive only from the census of 1841 onwards. These show that in Kelvedon Hatch there were 206 males and 223 females. The overwhelming number in employment were farm labourers or domestic servants. Village craftsmen included six sawyers, four carpenters, three blacksmiths and two wheelwrights. There was also a publican, church clerk, miller, butcher, baker, dealer, shopkeeper and schoolmistress. Up at Kelvedon Hall young squire Wright lived with his two brothers, all three in their twenties, waited on by seven servants. At Great Myles a Scottish widow with four children had nine servants and one more living out at the Lodge. The village priest with six children was grand enough to have a butler, as well as three servants. Brizes lacked a resident tenant at the time of the census but was occupied by six servants. At Germains Farm the old custom of having unmarried farm-workers live in with the family was still kept up. At Hall Cottage eleven members of the

106. End of an era – Ingatestone High Street in 1840. The cessation of coaching would rapidly reduce the town to a backwater.

C. SLOCOMBE'S
(Late RICHARDSON'S)
COMPANION
TO THE
ALMANACS for 1851.

Any corrections or suggestions for improvement in this Companion will be thankfully received and attended to by C. Slocombe, Ongar, Essex.

STONDON MASSEY CHURCH, ESSEX.
From a Drawing taken on the spot by Mr. Augustus Noble.
Reb. E. J. Reebe, Rector.

107. *Stondon Massey church depicted in Slocombe's almanac for 1851.*

108. *The parsonage at Stondon Massey.*

Sitch family were crowded in together. But only one person in the entire community is described as a pauper. Comparison with the two protestation oath lists of 1641-2 reveals that of the sixty-six different names recorded there only four are replicated in the census returns of 1841. Of these only the Barnes family can be proved to have been present in two generations. Their presence is confirmed by an entry in the burial register for 1813, recording the passing of John Barnes, aged 73, for 43 years clerk of the parish. The head of one Weal family was born in Kelvedon, the other in Stanford Rivers. The head of the White family was born in South Weald. The sole Baker was a male servant whose birthplace was unrecorded. All of which bespeaks a high degree of population mobility over the course of the previous two centuries.

By 1851 the population of Kelvedon Hatch had risen to its peak. There were 256 males but only 229 females, suggesting a degree of out-migration by the latter. The returns also give details of place of birth rather than just whether it was in Essex or outside England. The vast majority were still very much from the immediate locality but the Curate, who employed a London-born governess, was married to a Londoner and had one of his children born in Belgium, while the Rector's wife had been born in Denmark. In fact well over half (54) of the 87 households were headed by a person not born in Kelvedon, although thirty of them had been born very nearby,

in Navestock, Doddinghurst, Blackmore, Stondon or South Weald. Up at Kelvedon Hall Squire Wright, now a JP, had a Catholic priest staying as a house-guest and had taken on a butler. Ten people were recorded as receiving parish relief, one claiming to be 103 years of age. Two deaf-mute brothers were also recorded as well as a six year old 'idiot - dumb'. The village had also acquired a resident policeman.

The 1861 returns show a fall in population to 237 males and 217 females. Novel occupations included those of victualler, farrier, game-keeper, postman and basket-maker and grocer. The ten-strong Sawkins family were consigned to the 'Poor Houses', while a forty-six-year-old widow struggled as a laundress to support her five children. Squire Wright had taken on a maid from Cork and three Kellys from the same city had also settled in the village. Most surprising, however, is the advent of three Chelsea Pensioners, one aged seventy-five but the other two still only in their forties. Thirty-two residents were employed as domestic servants, less than a third of whom were born in Essex.

The following decade witnessed a further decline in population, to 223 men and 178 women. Following Squire Wright's death in 1865 Kelvedon Hall had passed to his nephew, Edward. He, his

mother and two sisters were waited on by eleven servants. At Brizes Mr Royds, a retired land-owner, lived with his Glaswegian wife and eleven servants. The Revd Fane at Priors was entertaining a visitor from Australia. A new resident was fifty-nine-year-old law reporter Alfred Clyatt, whose twenty-six-year-old wife had already borne him five children. Auctioneer Frederick Kent of Glover's Farm bested him with nine children, aged two to eighteen. The four cottages for the poor, built in the seventeenth century, were rented to four farm labourers and their families. In one of them George and Sarah Sarling survived with his infirm father and their eight offspring and one, presumably illegitimate, grandson. At the Shepherd Inn there lodged a pauper widow, a watchmaker, one of the deaf-mutes, now a widower, and his unmarried son. On the common Benjamin Fletcher, a travelling cutler, lived in a caravan which also served as his workshop.

By 1881 the population was down to 199 males and 176 females. An out-migration of the young and able-bodied was clearly discernible. Of the eighty-nine households seven were headed by widows, five by widowers, two each by retired persons or designated 'cripples' and one each by an invalid and an annuitant. Five more widows lived in with other families, as did two retired

109. All Saints Hutton church; pencil dawing of 1859.

110. *All Saints and St Faith, Childerditch – a pencil drawing dated 1859.*

111. *St Peter's, South Weald, c.1830.*

112. *The high altar in St Paul's church, Bentley.*

persons and an 'idiot' child. In all thirty-two households were headed by someone aged sixty or more. Under half (156) of the inhabitants had been born in Kelvedon, although another thirty-three had been born in Doddinghurst and a dozen in Navestock. The increased mobility of population was reflected in the fact that half a dozen residents had been born in Ireland and others in Bolton, Shrewsbury, Sheffield, Pontefract, Norwich and Guernsey. Of the most prolific families of 1841 – the Burton (11), Charge (8), Cooper (12), Firbank (8) Gold (8) Mott (6) Riglin (7) Stern (7) and Thomas (7) families had all left. There was only one Barnes left from seven and one Gandy from six, two Harringtons from eight and three Sawkins from ten. But there were still eight Beadles from ten, nine Sitches from twelve and ten Rainbirds and ten Sarlings from original families of sixteen; the impoverished Enevers had grown from fourteen to twenty-five and the Jarvises from six to twenty. Of these the Beadles, Enevers, Jarvises, Sarlings and Sawkins were all still labourers, while the Sitches and Rainbirds had risen into the ranks of the skilled.

ILL FARES THE LAND

The 'High Farming' prosperity of the mid-century which had supported capital-intensive investment in buildings and machinery and encouraged the agricultural engineers Burgess and Key to establish their works in Brentwood gave way to a profound malaise under the impact of cheap imported foodstuffs from the 1870s. While Brentwood itself continued to expand in size and population, its satellite villages contracted. The population of Navestock, which had peaked at 982 in 1851, fell to 692 over the following half century. Kelvedon Hatch declined from 502 to 361 over the same period. The burial register for that parish records stark indicators of social stress in the 1890s. In 1891 George Cooper, aged 42, was found with his throat cut, having previously tried to drown himself. (The cause may have been purely personal grief – a Leonard Cooper had been buried the previous year aged 7 months.) In 1892 George Harrington died of a fit at eighteen and Edward Weal at 54 "from the effects of drink". In 1895 Robert Knights, 25, was found dead in Cartshed Wood.

113. A late intruder - a view of 1909, one of the earliest depictions of a motor vehicle in Brentwood. The scene is of the crowd watching the fire which devastated Wilson's department store. The Hunter memorial is visible in the smoke.

Landowners were dismayed to see their rent rolls collapse. On the Petre estates arrears rose from an annual average of twenty-five pounds in 1870 to over fifteen hundred by 1893, despite overall rent reductions of forty per cent.

Some proprietors feared their farms might become entirely untenanted and revert to scrub. Such a prospect required bold measures. In 1884 Lord Petre's agent at Thorndon Park began to recruit farmers in Scotland, organising special trains to bring down not only their families and furniture but their equipment and livestock as well. In less than a decade he had fourteen farms under Scottish managers who abandoned traditional but unviable cereal crops in favour of hay, potatoes and dairying. Nor did this initiative lack imitators. The 1891 census showed fifty-eight Scottish farmers settled in the area of Brentwood and Ongar. Unlike their southern counterparts the Scots could usually count on their entire family to labour on the land rather than seek easier employment elsewhere. They also gained a reputation throughout the county as hard men in dealing with their labourers, though they were as hard on themselves, invariably working even longer hours than their men.

114. A traditional clapboard house in Brentwood High Street.

Schools

From Tudor times until the early nineteenth century educational provision in the Brentwood area was patchy and often discontinuous. Even the grammar school founded by Sir Anthony Browne would have been judged in modern terms "failing" through long periods of its history. Given the relative prosperity of the locality and the significant numbers of gentry among its population this paucity of provision might at first glance seem slightly surprising. But, given that many of the wealthier inhabitants were retirees, whose offspring were long past childhood, and that those who did have boys could afford to send them to a London school or Chigwell or Felsted or employ private tutors, any involvement by the gentry tended to be in the role of patron or governor of schools intended to cater for those of lower social standing than their own.

One pre-Reformation initiative is known to have proved abortive. Around 1500 John Andrew, a London ironmonger, built a chapel to our Lady at Redcrosse, on the London Road, near Honeypot Lane, probably hoping to tap into the pilgrim traffic. If so, the project failed because he converted the building into a school, which had closed by 1519, when he made his will.

The advent of Protestantism, with its emphasis on the Bible, and the growing monetisation and market-orientation of economic life combined to make literacy an increasingly desirable accomplishment. The growing value placed on education in Tudor society is evidenced by the will of William Butler, a husbandman rather than a member of the commercial classes, who bequeathed John Butler of St Leonard's in Fryerning "all my goods on condition that he shall bring up my son William virtuously with good and godly education and taught to write, read and cast accounts ...".

Brentwood School, founded by Sir Anthony Browne in 1557, was one of hundreds established throughout the land in the half century after the dissolution of the monasteries. Its first master was George Otway. His successor, John Greenwood (died 1609) was a man of some distinction, the author of *Syntaxis et Prosodia*. It was not until 1622, however, well over half a century since the school's foundation, that its statutes were finally enshrined in law.

It is known that by 1559 there was also a school-master living and teaching at Brook Street, because he was accused of failing to bring his pupils to church.

In 1591 the wife of William Clarke of South Weald who "teacheth a few children to read English" was told by the authorities to produce her licence or stop.

In 1641 Parliament required adult males to take a public oath of loyalty. The lists of signatories to these 'Protestation Oaths' provide a rough indicator of the most basic literacy among adult males – the ability to sign one's own name. Of sixty men who signed at Kelvedon Hatch thirty-five were obliged to sign with a cross.

The Society for the Promotion of Christian Knowledge in 1699 launched a movement to establish free charity schools where the children of the respectable poor could be instructed in basic literacy and numeracy and the principles of the Anglican faith. Fryerning had one and so did Ingatestone but both proved short-lived. Brentwood had a charity school for girls, founded by a gentlewoman, at least between 1714 and 1724. There were also two privately owned schools which taught surveying and other useful skills. At South Weald in 1726 twelve children were being taught to read at the expense of the vicar.

Parallel with this was a growth in private schools, catering to the needs and ambitions of an aspirant middle class. One at Shenfield appears to have been particularly 'progressive' having renounced corporal punishment and allocating each pupil a plot of ground to cultivate. The area's reputation for a health-giving environment and its relative proximity to the capital (to allow parental visits) combined with its relative distance from the capital (to banish metropolitan temptations) made it eminently suitable for such establishments.

Renewed impetus for provision came out of the Sunday School movement promoted by Gloucestershire newspaper-owner Robert Raikes in the 1780s. At one level its success may have reflected the growing strength of Evangelicalism, with its revival of the Puritan emphasis on Bible-study. At another it was a response to the facts of demography. Rapid population growth, especially among the labouring poor, who had no incentive to postpone reproduction, meant that there were undeniably and very visibly many more children around. In 1807 the local clergyman at Doddinghurst reported that he had tried to start a Sunday School but that it had failed within weeks and the only other educational provision in the village was an old woman who taught fifteen to twenty children to read. At East Horndon there was a private school for thirty-three infants and two small Catholic schools – supported by Lord and Lady Petre respectively – which also admitted non-Catholics. South Weald spawned a Sunday School for some two dozen local children, attached to St Peter's and by 1807 there was a 'school of industry' with thirty-two pupils as well. There were also three other day schools at South Weald, though these may have offered little more than a child-minding service for over-burdened parents. In 1818 the vicar, out of his own pocket, paid the parish clerk to act as master of both a day and Sunday school. In the same year a separate charity school for girls is known. They merged in 1839. By 1846 the school, supported by fees and donations, had a teacher's house and a hundred and twenty pupils. In the same year a school was built at Warley Hill, to the designs of S S Teulon.

A similar pattern obtained in Brentwood. A Sunday school was in existence by 1808 and a day industrial school a decade later. In 1835 a National school for girls was built and the decayed St Thomas's chapel became a school for boys in 1836. Supported by the Revd William Tower, master of Brentwood School, the latter soon gained a good reputation, despite irregular attendance. Another Sunday school, associated with the Congregationalists, was first recorded in 1808, developed into a day school and lasted until the 1870s. Two small Catholic schools, in existence by 1839, failed by 1845 but were soon revived as a single institution, St Helen's, housed from 1861 in the chapel formerly dedicated to that saint.

In 1856 Charles Belli, the long-serving vicar of South Weald, donated land opposite the church on which he built a new National (i.e. C of E) school, also to designs by Teulon. In 1864 Henry Moss of Bentley conveyed to trustees a newly built church school in Ashwells Road. In 1875 Belli gave more land, and with the support of Octavius Coope MP of Rochetts, built another infants' school in Crescent Road.

115. *St Thomas's Chapel, when used as a schoolroom.*

White's *Directory* provides an overview of local educational provision as it stood in 1848. Brentwood had its Grammar School, a National School and five other private schools. One of these had opened in 1820 and, variously located in High Street, Queen's Road and Rose Valley, survived for at least a century. At Blackmore there was a new (1841) infant school and a private ladies' school. Childerditch had acquired its National School in 1844 and there was another in Hutton. Ingatestone boasted two private 'academies' and there were four in Fryerning. Ingrave, thanks to the patronage of the Petres, had one school for Anglicans and two for Catholics. Shenfield had three ladies' boarding schools and a National School. Stondon Massey had a boarding school. Mountnessing had a charitable free school for the poor. However, the 1851 census figures show that, although there were two resident schoolmistresses at Kelvedon Hatch, of the fifty-four households with children aged five to fifteen only thirty-five officially mustered juveniles designated as 'scholar', while eighteen were listed as labourers or servants, one as young as seven. The sixty-four children not listed as either were presumably expected to help out at home.

By the 1860s Bawdes at Pilgrims Hatch was a private school, Gilstead Hall an academy, Pilgrims Hall and Wealdside at South Weald were both boarding schools and Serpents Hall housed a preparatory school.

Brentwood School was kick-started out of mediocrity by an Act of Parliament in 1851. The reformative Act was followed by an energetic building programme which provided new classrooms in 1853, a dormitory above Old Big School in 1855, more classrooms in 1865 and a chapel in 1867-8. A succession of able headmasters gradually expanded its numbers, its horizons and its achievements. Major new buildings were erected in 1909-10 and the school grounds extended thanks to the generosity of the chairman of the governors, Evelyn Heseltine. James ('Jimmy') Hough, headmaster 1914-45, acquired historic properties such as Barnards and Roden House, secured the admission of the school to the Headmasters' Conference and promoted a building programme which added a hall, library, laboratories, swimming bath, shooting range and squash courts. His career also embraced distinguished service in local government and charity work.

In 1854 the Shoreditch Agricultural and Industrial School was built in London Road to provide three hundred workhouse children with an alternative to the tutelage of Fagin and his ilk. In 1877 the institution came under the administration of a merged school district combining Shoreditch with Hackney. When this was dissolved in 1885 Hackney took it over, adding an infants' department. In 1894 one of the staff was imprisoned for cruelty to the children.

The Shoreditch initiative inspired imitators. In 1874 the London School Board opened an industrial school in Rose Valley, which lasted until 1902. In 1886 the diocese of Westminster established St Charles RC workhouse school for boys in Weald Road in the charge of the Brothers of Mercy, then *c*.1900 the Sisters of Charity and in 1936 the Irish Christian Brothers. It finally closed in 1954 and reopened in 1971 as a youth treatment

116. Brentwood School c.1905 note the protective fence around the Martyr's Elm.

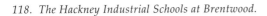

117. *The opening of new buildings at Brentwood School on the eve of the Great War. These represented the culmination of half a century of reform and expansion.*

118. *The Hackney Industrial Schools at Brentwood.*

119. *The Poplar Training School at Shenfield.*

120. *The croquet lawn at the Ursuline Convent.*

centre. In 1906-7 Hutton Industrial School was built over a hundred acre site by Poplar Board of Guardians at the initiative of its chairman, George Lansbury. The advent of its seven hundred and fifty youthful residents and ancillary staff trebled the population of Hutton.

The advent of state-sponsored education in the 1870s also began to provide grants for existing church schools – St Peter's, South Weald in 1873, Crescent Road in 1876, St Paul's, Ashwell's Road from 1893. But private enterprise continued to provide its own initiatives. Indeed, between 1826 and 1900, no less than twenty-nine private schools were listed in directories covering the Brentwood area. Establishments for boys were fewer but tended to last longer. Most were small, usually shifted sites and often changed names in the course of their existence. Whitelyons school, for example, began in the High Street in 1873, moved to Love Lane (Coptfold Road) a decade later and was optimistically renamed Hope House when it operated in Rose Valley a decade after that. In 1905 its enrolment was just twenty-five and by 1917 it had gone. In 1874 Brook House girls' school opened in South Weald and lasted until 1902. At about the same time Margaret Parlby started a girls' school in Brook Street which lasted some twenty years. In the 1880s a Miss Sarah Wills was running a school in Brook Street. In 1879 Kate Bryan built Montpelier House in Queen's Road as a girls' school. By 1905 it was reckoned the best establishment of its kind in Brentwood. In 1913 it was taken over by Essex County Council to become Brentwood County High School. It moved to Shenfield Common in 1927.

In 1895 a Mr Kenner founded Brentwood High School for Boys in Rose Valley. It survived until 1929. In 1900 the Ursuline Convent school opened with fifteen pupils in Queen's Road, where it still flourishes.

Brentwood's expanding population in the twentieth century was matched by expanding state provision, especially in the two decades after World War Two. Junction Road school originated in 1904. In 1910 Essex County Council opened New Road technical school, replaced by a senior school in 1936. In 1950 Pilgrim's Hatch school opened in Larchwood Gardens to cater for the children of the new Bishop's Hall estate and had to be enlarged as early as 1955. Hogarth junior and infant schools were opened in Shenfield in 1954-5. St Peter's Church of England school in Wigley Bush Lane was rebuilt in 1957-60 and enlarged in 1968. St Paul's Church of England

121. *George Lansbury MP, mayor of Poplar and Leader of the Labour Party.*

School in Ashwells Road was enlarged in 1958 and 1974. St Thomas of Canterbury and St Helen's RC Schools moved to new sites in Sawyers' Hall Lane in 1968 and 1973 respectively.

In 1962 Brentwood College of Education opened in Sawyers' Hall Lane. It later became the Chelmer Institute of Higher Education's Faculty of Education, then a part of Anglia Polytechnic University before the site was abandoned for redevelopment. In 1968 Brentwood Secondary School opened in Doddinghurst Road as the area's first comprehensive. Ingatesone's Anglo-European School opened in 1973 and in 1978 was Britain's first school to offer the International Baccalaureate examination.

Private establishments were not entirely extinguished, however, even in the twentieth century. In the 1920s Boyle's Court was leased to the wife of philosopher Bertrand Russell as home for a 'progressive' school, based on the sage's thinking. It moved to Petersfield in Hampshire in 1927, presumably to the relief of the neighbours. Less intrusively, no doubt, a Miss Duchesne continued to run a ladies' academy at The Hollies on Ingrave Road next to Wilson's Stores until the 1930s.

Scholars and Scholarship

COUNTRY CLERGY

Although the church's monopoly of higher learning was already being eroded by the Reformation, the link between priestly status and scholarly attainment long persisted, not least because many Oxbridge colleges had acquired the advowson of church livings which they used to provide for favoured dons. William Smith became vicar of Ingatestone in 1619 and in 1620 became rector of Fryerning as well. He held both posts simultaneously until 1630 when he resigned to become Vice Chancellor of the University of Oxford. A West Country man, Smith was also Warden of recently founded Wadham College.

Wadham chose almost every rector of Fryerning from 1620 onwards. St John's College, Cambridge presented to the living of Great Warley from the tenure (1708-43) of Henry Cardell onwards, though he was a former Fellow of Clare College. Cardell was the author of theological works, as was Hastings Robinson, rector from 1827 to 1866.

Although the relationship between colleges and country livings was capable of abuse it could also confer benefits. Remote rural areas acquired the services of clergy who were highly educated and capable of providing communal leadership. John Groome (1678-1760) vicar of Childerditch from 1709 until his death felt sufficiently strongly on the subject to publish in 1710 an octavo volume entitled *The Dignity and Honour of the Clergy represented in an Historical Collection : shewing how useful and serviceable the Clergy have been to this Nation by their universal learning, acts of charity and the administration of civil offices.* Groome died childless and left his library to his old Cambridge college, Magdalene. The bulk of his estate was left to fund scholarships at Magdalene for the benefit of the sons of Essex clergymen. He also thoughtfully left a stipend of six pounds a year to his successors to cover the costs of repairing to Cambridge annually to check that the scholarships had been filled.

Many country clergy were well off and prepared to use their resources for the benefit of their parishes and parishioners and, admittedly, themselves. Hastings Robinson was wealthy enough

122. Fairstead, built to supersede the Old Rectory at Great Warley.

to make successive improvements to the Old Rectory at Great Warley. In 1829 he spent £310 on "The building of a Water Closet and bedroom over the brewhouse, a forcing pump erected, the Coach House enlarged, a Shrubbery planted, new gravel walk laid out, drain made ... Necessary removed from the side of the House." The following year he spent £85 on a room to serve as a servants' hall and occasional lecture room. In 1831 he built a harness room and in 1832 a cowhouse. Over the following thirty years he spent in excess of a £1000 more adding a pantry, study, larder, workroom and greenhouse. After all that in 1888 Robinson's successor, Hammond Roberson Bailey, moved out and built the house known as Fairstead at his own expense. Bailey was distinguished as both a classicist and mathematician and took over after a teaching career at Cambridge and held the living until 1900.

Hastings Robinson (1792-1866) was very nearly an academic star. Educated at Rugby, at St John's College, Cambridge he progressed steadily through the ranks of BA and MA to become a fellow and assistant tutor in classics. He published an edition of Euripides *Electra* and a commentary on the *Acts of the Apostles* and in 1824 was elected a Fellow of the Society of Antiquaries. These achievements failed, however, to secure him the prestigious Regius Professorship of Greek, and so in 1827 Robinson was presented to the living of Great Warley which was in the gift of his college. The duties of such a post were far from onerous and afforded its holder ample time to continue with scholarly interests. Robinson's own chosen field became the English

Reformation and, in particular, the links between English bishops and the Protestant reformers in Switzerland during the reign of Elizabeth I. The pursuit of his enquiries took Robinson to Zurich to consult its archives, leading to the publication of four volumes of documentation between 1842 and 1847. As the railway was then only in its infancy in Europe Robinson's field work in Switzerland must have involved arduous journeys and prolonged absence from his parishioners. An earnest evangelical, he was also actively involved in the work of the Society for the Promotion of Christian Knowledge. Robinson died and was buried at Great Warley, after a tenure of almost forty years.

SCIENCE AND SPECULATION

Thomas Rutherforth (1712-71), some time rector of Shenfield and Regius Professor of Divinity at Cambridge, had an intriguingly paradoxical cast of mind. After graduating from St John's College, he taught science as a private tutor at Cambridge, published his lectures in an edition of two volumes and was elected a Fellow of the Royal Society. But he also qualified as a Doctor of Divinity and, in an age of increasing scepticism, became a noted theological controversialist, publishing treatises in defence of traditional church teachings on the efficacy of prophecy and the validity of miracles. Rutherforth also published a commentary on the pioneering work of the seventeenth century Dutch philosopher Hugo Grotius in developing international law. In addition to his Shenfield living, he also held another at Barley in Hertfordshire and additionally had the doubtless trying appointment of chaplain to the foul-tempered Frederick, Prince of Wales.

Samuel Horsley (1733-1806) who became vicar of South Weald in 1782, was the son of a clergyman and succeeded to his living as rector of Newington Butts, Surrey in 1759 and in 1777 to his position as lecturer at St Martin-in-the-Fields. Elected FRS in 1767, he became one of its secretaries in 1773.

Throughout the 1780s Horsley deployed his great learning and considerable powers of invective to rubbish the theological writings of the dissenter Joseph Priestley, who was incidentally the discoverer of oxygen. In 1783 Horsley was invited to join The Club established by Dr Johnson, which included Reynolds, Goldsmith and Burke among its luminaries. Horsley subsequently became embroiled with Sir Joseph Banks, President of the Royal Society, in a dispute about its

123. *Salute to a scientist – memorial to Francis Wollaston by the eminent sculptor Sir Francis Chantrey.*

management which became so acrimonious that Horsley finally resigned. In 1785 Horsley published an edition of the works of Sir Isaac Newton which he had been working on since 1779. In the course of his investigations he discovered 'a cartload' of Newton's manuscripts on religious topics but ignored them as unworthy of publication. Horsley subsequently served as bishop of St David's, Rochester and St Asaph's.

Francis Wollaston (1762-1823) became vicar of South Weald in 1794, two years after being elected Jacksonian professor at Cambridge where he was said to present no less than three hundred scientific experiments a year. In the same year he published his lectures on chemistry. In 1807 he was made Master of his old college Sydney Sussex but was deprived of his position within a year because he had never been a Fellow and was therefore technically ineligible for the post. Despite also being appointed rector of Cold Norton and East Dereham and archdeacon of Essex Wollaston continued to reside at South Weald until his death. The marble medallion sculpted in his memory by Sir Francis Chantrey bears the inscription "He went to bed in perfect health October 11th 1823 and was found a corpse on Sunday morning. Reader reflect."

MASTERS OF MUSIC

Purely scholarly preoccupations came late in life to Maurice Greene (?1696-1755) whose career was largely devoted to music as a practical profession at the highest level. He became organist of St Paul's Cathedral in his twenties and in 1727 organist and composer to the Chapel Royal as well. In 1730 he was appointed Professor of Music at Cambridge and in 1735 Master of the King's Band of Music. By the age of forty therefore he had accumulated the four chief appointments in music in the country. In 1738 Greene helped to found the Royal Society of Musicians. A German work published in 1739 numbered Greene among the most eminent organists in Europe, a compliment given to no other Englishman. In 1750 he inherited Bois Hall, Navestock from the bastard son of his uncle. With it came an annual income of £700. This enabled him to devote the last five years of his life to collecting and editing manuscripts of church music, both English and foreign. Greene's own compositions included a setting of Pope's *Ode on St Cecilia's Day*, a course of lessons for aspirant harpsichord players, two oratorios, cantatas for royal marriages and numerous anthems, ballads, songs and organ voluntaries.

Musicologist Edward Taylor (1784-1863), son of a noted hymn-writer of Norwich, switched from engineering to music when he was forty-three years old. Although his training in music had been informal and limited, he could play the organ, oboe and flute and in 1824 had organised an entire music festival in his native city, as well as training the choir. His other assets included a rich bass voice, a commanding presence and the friendship of the German composer Spohr, whose works he translated for performance in England, along with several of Haydn and Mozart. From 1829 to 1843 he was music critic of the *Spectator*. In 1837 Taylor was appointed Professor of Music at Gresham College in London, a post he held until his death, which occurred at his home, Gresham Cottage, Cornslands Road, Brentwood. He was laid to rest in the old dissenting-ground in King's Road.

DILENTTANTI OF THE HYDE

Thomas Hollis (1720-74) was originally intended for commerce but, inheriting two fortunes, opted to study under John Ward (?1679-1758) the antiquarian, FRS and Professor of Rhetoric at Gresham College. Hollis then made two lengthy Grand Tours of Europe, before eventually settling at The Hyde, Fryerning. He then devoted much of his time and fortune to the promotion of his libertarian principles by buying or produc-

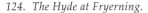

124. The Hyde at Fryerning.

125. *Thomas Hollis*

126. *Thomas Brand Hollis.*

ing books and commemorative medals "for the purpose of illustrating and upholding liberty, preserving the memory of its champions, to render tyranny and its abettors odious". These he presented to learned institutions and libraries, from Harvard to Zurich. In 1764 he presented Sydney Sussex College, Cambridge with a portrait of its most famous alumnus, Cromwell. A recluse and non-churchgoer, Hollis was branded a republican and an atheist, although he thought of himself as merely an ardent Whig and his memoirs show him to have been a man of deep personal piety. He not only eschewed drinking in an age devoted to alcoholic excess but also abstained from salt, sugar, spices, butter and even milk. Hollis personally edited at least nine publications, including works by or about Milton, Sidney, Plato and Locke.

When Hollis died he left his home, collections and fortune to his friend, Thomas Brand who thenceforth styled himself Thomas Brand-Hollis. Sharing Hollis's Whiggish principles, Brand-Hollis was very much the activist, rather than the recluse. In 1780 he was one of the leading signatories of an Essex declaration of opposition to the war against the American colonists. He became a friend of John Adams, future president

and first diplomatic representative of the USA when it achieved its independence. Adams visited The Hyde in 1786 to be greeted by busts of Plato and Marcus Aurelius and wonder at a classical temple in the gardens.

John Disney (1779-1857) founder of the Cambridge University chair of archaeology called by his name, was the eldest son of the Rev. John Disney D.D. (1746-1816), an energetic Unitarian minister and religious controversialist who had in 1804 been bequeathed estates to the annual value of £5000, including the Hyde. This mighty windfall at once induced the elder Disney to abandon his ministrations at the Unitarians' Essex Street chapel, off the Strand, and to take up residence at the Hyde and dabble in literature and agriculture, while enjoying the collection of classical antiquities amassed in Italy by his benefactor, Thomas Brand Hollis, between 1748 and 1753. Inheriting his father's estate in 1816, John Disney added to the collection of antiquities, initially through a relative who acquired items from Pompeii, and later by himself visiting Rome. He then compiled a systematic catalogue of the Museum Disneianum, published in three volumes between 1846 and 1849. Disney's enthusiasm, however, appears to have exceeded his critical faculties. An engraving of what is clearly a mirror with a handle, for example, is captioned as a stew-pan. Despite his friendship with Flaxman, the most knowledgeable classical sculptor of the day, Disney also appears to have bought some very dud marbles. The best, however, went to the Fitzwilliam Museum at Cambridge, where they formed an important element of its core collection. Disney endowed the Cambridge chair with £1000 in 1851, adding a further £3,250 on his death. A successful barrister and published author on electoral law, he was honoured by the university with an honorary doctorate of laws. He was also a Fellow of the Royal Society.

FOUNDING FATHERS

The antiquary James Ford (1779-1850), a fellow of Trinity College, Oxford became vicar of Navestock in 1830, the year in which he married the daughter of an Ipswich bookseller. Ford collected materials to update Morant's pioneering and comprehensive *History of Essex* but never managed to write it, although he did publish two volumes of popular theology. Dying childless, he left careful instructions for "a funeral of great simplicity." He also left £2000 to fund a Ford's Professorship of English History at Oxford and left Trinity College £4000 to purchase advowsons and another £4000 for four Ford's Studentships (i.e. undergraduate scholarships).

William Stubbs (1825-1901) was plucked from obscurity, only to be returned to it, seemingly denied the academic destiny for which he was so eminently qualified. A poor widow's son, of Yorkshire yeoman stock, Stubbs was obliged to pay his way through his undergraduate studies at Christ Church, Oxford by working as a part-time college servant. This lowly occupation compromised him socially and barred him from a teaching post in college once he had graduated. Trinity took him on briefly as a fellow but in 1850 he left to succeed Ford as vicar of Navestock, a living in the gift of the college. For the next fifteen years he was a conscientious pastor and liked to claim in later years that he "knew every toe on every baby in the parish". Stubbs married the village schoolmistress, Catherine Dellar, daughter of a local man. The vicar's kindness and geniality certainly won him the affection of his flock, but meanwhile he toiled to win academic recognition as an historian. The *Dictionary of National Biography* speaks of him as utilising "his leisure as a village parson" but seems to overlook the fact that, apart from his pastoral duties, he

127. William Stubbs. Later to be bishop of Oxford, he married the Navestock schoolmistress.

also had a growing family – eventually five sons and a daughter – to distract him. Nevertheless, as the *DNB* observes, he acquired "such a knowledge of the sources for English medieval history as made him the foremost scholar of his generation." In 1852 he became a founder member of the Essex Archaeological Society. In 1858 ten years labour came to fruition in Stubbs' first scholarly publication, a volume of tables setting out the succession to each episcopal see in England. This, like so many of Stubbs' laboriously achieved studies, would prove an invaluable basic tool for later generations of researchers. Next came careful editions of medieval documents, with copious notes clarifying their obscurities and prefatory essays setting them in context. Stubbs began to contribute articles to the *Archaeological Journal* but also took on extra burdens as a Poor Law guardian and diocesan inspector of schools. In addition he took on private pupils, including the poet Algernon Swinburne, then an undergraduate referred to Stubbs by the formidable Jowett of Balliol.

Release finally came in 1862 when Archbishop Longley appointed Stubbs to the post of librarian at Lambeth Palace, a virtual sinecure which not only gave him time for study but also free run of a treasure-house of primary source material. Stubbs continued, however, to reside at Navestock. Passed over for an Oxford chair that same year and again the following year, in 1866 he was finally appointed to the prestigious Regius Chair and at last moved back to Oxford. His magisterial *Constitutional History of England* was published between 1873 and 1878 and in 1888 he was made bishop of Oxford – his cathedral being the chapel at Christ Church, the university's largest, richest and most prestigious college, where he had once waited at table.

UNTO THIS LAST

The greatest literary success of Richard Francis Weymouth (1822-1902) came posthumously with the publication of his *New Testament in Modern Speech*, composed in the last decade of his life, during his retirement at Collaton House, Brentwood. By 1909 it was already in its third edition. A Devon man and graduate of University College, London, Weymouth supported his family as a schoolmaster while continuing to study and publish. He joined the Philological Society in 1851, contributed many papers to its *Transactions* and sat on its council. In 1868 he became the first person to be awarded a doctorate in literature by the University of London after completing a rigorous examination in Anglo-Saxon, English, Icelandic and French. No such degree was to be awarded again for more than a decade. The year after he achieved his doctorate Weymouth was elected a fellow of University College and appointed headmaster of Mill Hill, a nonconformist foundation then reorganising itself on public school lines. A zealous Baptist, a strict disciplinarian, an effective administrator and a sound teacher, Weymouth successfully increased the school's intake before retiring with a pension in 1886. He had managed to maintain his scholarly output by publishing a study of *Early English Pronunciation, with Especial reference to Chaucer*, but was now free to devote himself entirely to study. Gladstone, himself a classicist of note, greatly admired Weymouth's scholarship and in 1891 secured him a civil list pension of £100 a year. Weymouth's first wife and the mother of his six children died that year. He retired to Brentwood the following year to complete his magnum opus, remarrying within a twelvemonth.

A Wider World – Travellers and Adventurers

OLD SALTS

Captain John Troughton (d.1621), son of a York baker, served in the household of Sir John Petre as a page before going to sea. In 1590 he was involved in the capture of the *Spiritus Sanctus* en route to the East Indies and in 1600 captained the *Lioness* with orders to curb English privateering in the Mediterranean. He seems to have interpreted these orders rather freely, himself indulging in engagements against the Spanish and Portuguese. In 1601 he seized the cargo of a Portuguese ship but was subsequently judged to have acted illegally. Although he was discharged he evidently felt uneasy enough about it to leave a bequest to the children of the Lisbon merchant whose goods he had seized. Returning home Troughton apparently retained the overbearing manner of a freebooter, being reported in 1602 for striking the collector for the poor with a walking stick – in church. In retirement he became a member of the first Lord Petre's household at Thorndon Hall. A fine portrait bust of Troughton can be found in the south aisle of Ingatestone church, a work attributed to the splendidly named Epiphanius Evesham.

Despite the fact that John Jervis (1735-1823) was the son of an Admiralty solicitor and treasurer of Greenwich Hospital for seamen, he entered the navy as an ordinary able seaman at fourteen, with twenty pounds from his father, who thereafter refused him any further aid. Jervis applied himself assiduously to mastering his profession, habitually using periods of leave to travel and acquaint himself with the harbours, coasts and navies of Europe. He first came to prominence in 1782 as commander of the eighty gun *Foudroyant*, when in a night action, he severely mauled and took the French seventy-four gunner *Pegase*, with negligible casualties. He was immediately made a Knight of the Bath. In 1783 he was at last able to marry his cousin, Martha, daughter of Sir Thomas Parker (?1695-1784), Chief Baron of the Exchequer, who lived at Rochetts, which thereafter became the home of the newlyweds.

Jervis's hour of glory came in 1797 off Cape St Vincent, when with 15 ships, he thwarted a Spanish fleet of 27, which was intending to join

128. Home for a Hero – Rochetts, home of Earl St Vincent.

up with a French fleet to effect an invasion of England. Four Spanish ships were taken and the rest fled, many badly damaged. The king made his victorious commander Earl St Vincent and Parliament voted him a handsome pension of £3000 a year. In the same year the newly ennobled admiral dealt severely with threatened mutinies by hanging ringleaders without mercy.

Forced from active command by failing health, St Vincent was appointed First Lord of the Admiralty and by a painstaking inspection of shore establishments revealed an appalling catalogue of theft, waste, corruption and inefficiency. Unsurprisingly this made him extremely unpopular and cost him his position. The admiral returned briefly to active service in 1806-7 and made his last contribution to a House of Lords debate in 1810. Sheridan hailed his retirement into private life as being crowned "with his triple laurel, over the enemy, the mutineer and the corrupt."

St Vincent's life in retirement at Rochetts was governed by the same passion for order and routine which had marked his naval career. Between 1809 and 1812 he served as one of the surveyors of the highways for South Weald, though he may well have paid a deputy to do much of the actual work. He did take a close personal interest in his estate, which sometimes led to friction with his neighbours, not that the admiral would have cared. A martinet, severe even by the brutal standards of his day, he had never worried about being unpopular. In 1816 the then youthful C T Tower initiated a case against him for cutting some underwood, valued at £34; Tower's solicitor's bill came to just over three thousand.

The admiral entertained hospitably, the Prince of Wales being a notable visitor. In 1821 the Prince marked his coronation as George IV by promoting St Vincent to the highest of naval ranks, Admiral of the Fleet. St. Vincent died two years later and the earldom died with him. Rochetts passed to his niece, Miss Jervis, who was still living there in 1848. It later became the home of Octavius Edward Coope of the Romford brewing family.

ADVENTURERS RETURNED

Donald Campbell of Barbreck (1751-1804) was one of that army of adventurous Scots who forsook his native soil in search of fortune. He made his way to India via Belgium, the Tyrol, Venice, Alexandria, Aleppo, Mosul, Bombay and Goa,

129. Memorial to John Tower in St Peter's church, South Weald. He was formerly an 'Admiral of the Blue' and a Companion to the Order of the Bath.

was shipwrecked in the Indian Ocean and imprisoned by Hyder Ali, ruler of Mysore and an ally of the French. Campbell was eventually released and served as commander of a cavalry regiment in the army of the Nawab of the Carnatic. In 1795 Campbell, safely returned, published an account of his odyssey and adventures in the form of a series of letters to his son. The book proved to be a considerable success, running to six editions by 1808. Campbell died at Hutton in 1804.

Sir John Hawker English (1788-1840) became surgeon-in-chief to the Swedish army and was decorated with the order of Gustavus Vasa while still only 25 but did not fully qualify as a doctor until after leaving Sweden, graduating MD from Gottingen in 1814. He was knighted by the Prince Regent in 1815 and from 1826 resided at Warley House, which had been built in 1805-6 to house the commandant of Warley barracks. He died at the newly-built resort of St Leonard's-on-Sea.

Lorne Road cemetery is the final resting-place

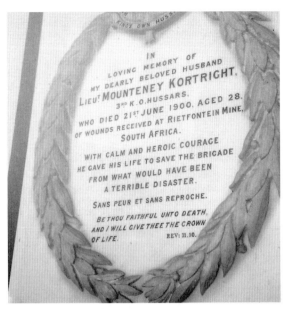

131. Fallen Hero Lt M. Kortright of Fryerning died of wounds while serving with the King's Own 3rd Hussars in the Boer War.

130. The gravestone of Michael Fleming in Lorne Road cemetery. Formerly a sergeant in the Irish Guards, he was accidentally killed while on duty during 'The Troubles' in Ireland.

of Sergeant James Owens (1827-1901), one of the earliest winners of the Victoria Cross. Born in County Cavan, Owens served with the 49th Regiment in the Crimea and won the award as a corporal for his actions at Sebastopol on 30 October 1854 where he "greatly distinguished himself in a personal encounter with the Russians and gave assistance to a lieutenant of his regiment".

Arthur Jephson (1858-1908) was born in the Rectory at Hutton, the fifth and youngest son of the vicar of Childerditch. Educated at Tonbridge School, he served aboard *HMS Worcester* alongside a young Japanese trainee, the future Admiral Togo, who was to destroy the Russian Baltic fleet in the Straits of Tsushima in 1905. Jephson's future, however, lay in Africa. After serving in the Royal Irish Rifles, in 1887 he enlisted with Henry Morton Stanley's expedition to 'rescue' Emin Pasha (Eduard Schnitzer), the German doctor appointed by General Gordon as governor of Egypt's Equatorial Province (i.e. Sudan). Gordon and the garrison he commanded at Khartoum, capital of

the Sudan, had been massacred by the Muslim army of the prophetic Mahdi in 1885. It was assumed that a similar fate awaited Gordon's subordinates elsewhere. Emin, a brilliant linguist, busily writing important geographical papers and despatching samples of plants and animals to Europe, was, however, unaware that he needed to be rescued. When, however, Jephson himself was entrusted to cross Lake Albert on the final phase of the journey and bring Emin to Stanley the governor complied. It was then decided that the Equatorial Province should be evacuated and Emin, accompanied by Jephson, was set to accomplish this. As it turned out Emin's troops rebelled against him rather than be rescued and both Emin and Jephson were imprisoned and sentenced to death. Jephson managed to escape and rejoin Stanley and together they returned to rescue Emin. Jephson returned safely to England in 1890 and was awarded a medal for his endeavours by the Royal Geographical Society. His account of his exploits *Emin Pasha and the Rebellion at the Equator* appeared in English, French and German editions. He followed this with a volume of African folk-tales. In 1895 Jephson entered yet another career as a Queen's Messenger. Emin Pasha, meanwhile, had returned to Africa only to be murdered by Arab slavers.

132. *Brentwood High Street c.1870. Note the new (1864) Town Hall with projecting clock on the left side.*

The Growing Town

URBANISATION

Physically, late-Victorian Brentwood's town centre began to lose its 'Olde Worlde' air. A parade of shops at 1-23 High Street was built by a Mr Spurgeon who bankrupted himself in the process. (The parade was torn down in 1972 and Halford's now occupies its site.) In 1883 Wilson & Co. opened as a boot and shoe retailer, moving into its prominent corner site on Ingrave Road as an emporium in 1889. Twenty years later 'Wilson's Great Eastern Stores' burned down after a fire started in a paint store. The local brigade, aided by troops from Warley barracks, contained the disaster and the store was quickly rebuilt in its present form.

In 1889 also a new station opened at Shenfield to service the new branch line to Southend. Despite its increasing urbanisation Brentwood still retained its reputation as a health-giving location. A Brentwood Convalescent Home for Children was founded in 1889. In 1892 Brentwood High Street acquired a new Post Office building. A

telephone exchange opened in 1899, the year in which the town achieved the status of an Urban District Council. In 1902 a purpose-built fire station opened in Hart Street. The census of 1901 revealed, however, that with a population of 4,932 Brentwood was still less populous than South Weald, which had 5,933 inhabitants.

In 1904 the Ilford photographic factory opened out at Great Warley, providing an important new source of employment. In 1912 the Brook Park estate was sold off for development as housing and a new sewerage works was opened in Nag's Head Lane at Brook Street. In 1914 the Palace cinema, Brentwood's first, was converted from Charter's drapery shop.

For some, evidently, the pace of change was threatening to become too fast.

A Committee of Conservators was established to protect Shenfield Common as early as 1884 and in 1890 The Avenue was planted as a make-work scheme for the unemployed. In 1902 Squire Tower of South Weald was instrumental in securing the preservation of the neglected ruins of St Thomas's chapel and having them enclosed with handsome railings.

For all that many of its residents commuted to London or elsewhere to work, late Victorian

133. *The fire which destroyed Wilson's store in 1909.*

134. *Brentwood High Street c.1907, showing the George and Dragon on the left and the White Hart on the right.*

135. *Brentwood High Street early 20th century. The absence of motor cars enables cyclists to travel abreast.*

136. *Brook Street Hill c.1906 – notice the unmetalled road surface.*

Brentwood and its environs still had far more the character of a small market town than a dormitory suburb. It had a rich associational life, expressed through dozens of flourishing clubs and societies. In 1886 a Volunteer Drill Hall opened in Ongar Road and in 1900 a Brentwood and District Mechanics' Institute was founded. The local 'harmonic society' dated back to the 1860s and a vocal and instrumental society was founded in 1880. In 1906 these were joined by Brentwood Operatic Society. The town also boasted a rather less conventional assemblage in Ye Old Original Brentwood Tramps' Band with over thirty members, which played in the local carnival and at fund-raising events for local charities

Religion also flourished in a variety of guises, with congregations vying to accommodate themselves in new buildings of style and substance. In 1881 the Church of the Holy Cross opened in Warley. In 1883 St Thomas's in Brentwood was rebuilt. In 1886 a Baptist church was established. A new Methodist Church on Warley Hill was built in 1892, and in 1895 a new St Nicholas

138. Shen almshouses, opened in 1910 by Brentwood School benefactor Evelyn Heseltine.

137. St Mary the Virgin, Great Warley, a spectacular church designed by Townsend.

139. *Warley Road c.1909.*

140. *Ingatestone High Street from the north-east.*

141. Borland Road, typical of many semi-residential thoroughfares in lacking paving and lighting.

142. The Great Eastern Railway Cycling Club at Kelvedon Hatch.

church, Kelvedon Hatch was consecrated. The architect was a local resident, John Newman FRIBA and his choice of style the avant-garde Arts and Crafts mode.

The most striking venture was, however, a matter of individual rather than institutional initiative. The church of St Mary the Virgin at Great Warley was dedicated in 1904, having been built at the expense of Evelyn Heseltine in memory of his brother Arthur, who had died in 1897. The architect, Charles Harrison Townsend (1851-1928), a leading light of the Art Workers' Guild, had recently gained national attention with the completion of three important public commissions in London – the Bishopsgate Institute, Whitechapel Art Gallery and the Horniman Museum. The influential German art critic Herman Muthesius hailed Townsend as the prophet of a novel modernity, ranking him alongside C F Voysey. St Mary the Virgin, however, eschews the idiosyncratic Art Nouveau of Townsend's three London creations in favour of

a mildly quirky exercise in Early English – at least on the outside. The fabulous interior of the church was the work of Sir William Reynolds-Stephens (1862-1943) and features organic forms, notably a recurrent poppy motif, emblematic of life and death, and an eclectic use of richly textured and exotic materials ranging from oxidised silver to galvanised iron, from teak, walnut and aluminium to marble and mother-of-pearl. Stephens later became President of the Royal Academy. Evelyn Heseltine also built the Shen Place Almshouses in 1910.

SPORT

Throughout the late Victorian period sport continued to increase in importance as a feature of English social life. In prosperous Brentwood and its environs its manifestations were appropriately bourgeois, even in some respects aristocratic. In 1882 a single day's bag in Weald Park amounted to 417 pheasants, 1,081 rabbits and four hares. In 1887 the Priory Polo Club was established at Hutton Hall. There was also steeplechasing at Childerditch. Little Warley golf club was established in 1899, with a nine-hole course and sixty members. The cycling craze of the 1880s led to the formation of a club large enough to warrant the publication of its own 'gazette' and there was also an athletic association with a large membership. There were local cricket clubs at Mountnessing and Ingatestone and Fryerning but Brentwood Cricket Club was reckoned to be one of the strongest Essex sides, being able to call on several county players, including the splendidly named Essex captain C J Kortright (1871-1952). In the 1890s 'Korty' was reckoned the fastest bowler in the world, although he never played for England. Nor, apparently, did he ever do a day's work in his life, having ample means to devote himself to cricket and, later, golf. Korty was eventually to be buried at Fryerning. Nearby lies Alfred 'Bunny' Lucas, another Essex captain who, in 1880, shared with W G Grace the distinction of making the first ever century partnership in Test cricket. Lucas also had the distinction of being captain of Essex in 1894, the year in which the team achieved first class county status. The graves of Kortright and Lucas are not, as tradition long held, exactly twenty-two yards apart – but one has to allow for Korty's run-up.

THE GARDENER AT WARLEY PLACE

The national passion for spade and trowel was vibrantly alive in the locality. A Brentwood Horticultural Society was founded *c.* 1872. In the 1880s its annual shows were held at Middleton Hall, then the home of Countess Tasker. Out at Warley Place at that time Miss Ellen Willmott (1858-1934) was creating one of the world's great gardens. The Willmott family settled there in 1876. Ellen's first project, a rock garden, was laid out by specialist contractors brought in all the way from York. When she began a new Alpine garden her father bought her another 22 acres to work on. In 1890 Ellen bought a chateau near Aix-les-Bains and began to create another great garden there. In 1905 she would buy yet another garden, in Italy. In 1907 her French property was badly damaged by fire; although it was uninsured she spent lavishly to restore it.

Gertrude Jekyll, doyenne of garden designers, explicitly deferred to Ellen in print as "the greatest of living women gardeners". Considering the number of hybrids now known as Willmottiae or Warleysii posterity has apparently endorsed this verdict. In 1897 Willmott and Jekyll were both awarded the Royal Horticultural Society's pres-

143. *Kings Road, c.1907.*

Kings Road, Brentwood.

144. The Music Room at Warley Place.

tigious Victoria Medal of Honour. Jekyll collected the award for both of them. Typically Ellen Willmott was abroad, collecting plants and devouring other people's gardens. On her seventh birthday she had come down to breakfast to find a cheque for a thousand pounds on her plate, the first of many such sent by her godmother, Helen Tasker. Ellen Willmott had money and spent it. Her music room was filled with instruments of all kinds, which she played with skill and enthusiasm. She liked working in wood and metal and shared Gertrude Jekyll's fascination with tools and gadgets. She was also a keen photographer, had her own darkroom and illustrated her first book *Warley Place in Spring and Summer* with her own black and white plates. Later she would be elected a fellow of the Linnaean Society and win four consecutive RHS Gold Medals for her daffodils.

The Warley garden at its peak employed more than eighty gardeners, cultivating and weeding its fifty acres. The team was multi-national, including Dutch, Swiss and Italians, chosen for their specific expertise. While resident abroad, Miss Willmott insisted on regular reports from Warley on the progress and problems of each area of the garden. It sounds obsessive and it was. Some sort of nemesis was inevitable. In 1910 she published an ambitious, lavishly illustrated volume on roses which proved to be a financial disaster. Warley had to be let and the head gardener discharged. The Italian property was also let. She sold off family treasures, including violins by Amati and Stradivarius, and took out a mortgage to enable her to hold on to her Italian property. Then came the war. The army took over the Warley estate and the rose collection simply disintegrated. During the 1920s she was elected to the Flora and Lily Committees of the RHS and awarded a medal by the National Rose Society but her staff had to go, the weeds advanced, the house got colder. In 1933 Ellen Willmott stood beside the grave of her friend, Gertrude Jekyll. A year later she was in her own grave, having died all alone. Her great garden reverted to wilderness. Warley Place and her belongings were auctioned off. A spring-time blaze of crocuses yet recalls her ardent spirit.

THE BLAST OF WAR
In August 1914 the heir to the throne was billeted at Warley Barracks with the Grenadier Guards. In 1915 new battalions would be raised there for the Irish and Welsh Guards.

A postcard sent from Brentwood in September 1914 recorded with excitement that "we saw train-loads of soldiers go through Brentwood station the other day. I expect they were going to Harwich. We heard the blackberries had been poisoned by German spies at South Weald but of course that is only a rumour."

The transformation of Brentwood "into one vast garrison" was vividly recalled by Frank Simpson, then a greatly excited small boy: "a military camp was set up on Shenfield Common and the Highwood Hospital was occupied by the military and the Poplar schools became the temporary home of the Duke of York's school evacuated from Dover and almost every household had one or more soldiers billeted upon them. Army

146. *Brentwood's Great War memorial in Lorne Road cemetery. Its base reads: 'This Cross of Sacrifice is one in design and intention with those which have been set up in France and Belgium and other places throughout the world where our dead of the Great War are laid to rest.'*

145. *Cyclists, clad in the approved fashions of the 1890s, pass the Bull Inn, Brook Street.*

147. Brentwood High Street at the beginning of the 20th century.

148. Cyclists and horse in the yard of the Old White Hart, Brentwood.

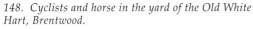

mule-waggons appeared to be everywhere and motor ambulances, some fitted with balloon like containers carried on the roof, which enabled them to operate on town-gas, could often be seen, as several of the large houses around the town were converted into military hospitals and war injured soldiers in 'hospital blue' became a common sight in the town."

The numbers were, indeed, very great. Between November 1914 and March 1919, 2,140 wounded passed through Coombe Lodge in Great Warley alone. The turnover must have been rapid, since it had only 83 beds plus an isolation tent in the garden. Graves in the disused cemetery at Lorne Road give some slight indication of the huge numbers of servicemen who came through Brentwood in the course of the conflict.

In 1916 the Army also took over Selo's photographic factory and retained it until 1921. Members of the newly-established Women's Auxiliary Army Corps were stationed out at Warley, where Sir John French came to cast an appreciative eye over them in 1917. German prisoners-of-war were set to work on local farms.

A Zeppelin flew over Brentwood in March 1916 but ignored it as a target. The only bomb to be dropped on Shenfield killed a Nurse Evans, ironically home on leave from duty in France.

149. *Shops in the High Street, 1906. The shop in the centre is run by a Mrs Austin.*

150. *The Old Swan Inn, Brentwood c.1906, showing the redundant archway for coaches.*

151. *The bandstand on Shenfield Common.*

152. *Shenfield High Street.*

The war memorials of the locality bear silent testimony to a measure of collective sacrifice which bore hardest on the forces' junior leadership. In 1915 Lionel, sixteenth Lord Petre, was killed in action as a Lieutenant with the Coldstream Guards. In 1916 Captain H P Fry, who had been born in Brentwood but had emigrated to Western Australia to become a grazier, was killed at Gallipoli. Memorials in Fryerning church honour the memory of Captain Gordon Elton of the Irish Fusiliers, who won the DSO and was killed in 1917 and Lieutenant P A Christy of the Essex Regiment who served on the Marne and the Aisne and in Flanders before being killed at the age of nineteen.

Brentwood's dead were commemorated by a memorial hospital extension, opened on 29 January 1921 and a memorial cross unveiled on 9 October the same year. The cost of these two projects – £6500 – was paid for by public subscription. The cross was designed by local architect A E Hill and built by Arthur Pilgrim & Sons.

INTER WAR

The two decades after the ending of the Great War witnessed the resumption of pre-war trends towards a lifestyle that was more mobile, more commercial and less sedate. Those who deplored these trends could find new refuge in the Thorndon Park golf club, founded in 1920. Members occupied a number of the grander ground floor rooms of Thorndon Hall which had finally been abandoned by the Petres as the estate was sold off in two major disposals. Lionel Petre's widow, remarried as Lady Rasch, devoted herself to the task of restoring the family's ancestral home, Ingatestone Hall.

The publication of the first edition of the *Brentwood Gazette* in 1919 was a milestone in the town's development, marking it as a community now large enough to generate its own news. Public facilities were enlarged with the opening of a new parish hall in Shenfield in 1922 and the Parade cinema next to Brentwood station the same year. Local bus services began in 1920 courtesy of the quaintly named National Steam Car Co. and by 1925 plans were already being mooted for an orbital road. Along the Ongar Road the Marconi company erected tall radio towers. In the High

153. A social event at Ingatestone Hall, c.1930.

154. The Parade cinema near Brentwood railway station.

Street old-established family businesses acquired new neighbours from the wider world of commerce as a branch of the Midland Bank was built in 1921, to be joined by Sainsbury's in 1924, the National Provincial Bank in 1927 and Woolworth's in 1930. Local employment was boosted in 1921 by the re-opening of the Selo/Ilford works at Great Warley to produce cine and X-ray film but in 1923 Burgess and Key's Victoria Works were sold to A E Symes for use as a builder's yard.

The pace of change quickened further in the 1930s. In 1930 the former Hackney Union Branch Workhouse and Infants School metamorphosed into St Faith's Hospital, specialising in the treatment of epileptics. In 1933 two additional tracks were laid between Shenfield and Gidea Park and Brentwood station was reconstructed. That same year Princess Mary came to lay the foundation stone for a new Brentwood District Hospital on land donated by Percy Bayman. Local fund-raising events garnered £40,000 towards the project. The hospital opened in 1934 and in 1937 John Logie Baird, the inventor of television, presented the hospital with a set, making it the first hospital in the world to have this facility for patients. In 1932 Ingatestone acquired a new church for Catholic worship, dedicated to SS John and Erconwald. In 1934 Brentwood gained a new

155. Brentwood Cottage Hospital.

Anglican church, St George's, the work of a local architect, Laurence King.

To meet increased local demand a new telephone exchange was opened in Queen's Road in 1932. The gas works in St James's Road closed. Out at Thoby Priory the sixteenth-century house built for the Berners family was abandoned and in 1937 the Chequers Inn in Brentwood High Street, which had been built around 1769, was

156. *Brentwood District Hospital.*

157. *St George's church, Ongar Road, built in 1934 to the designs of a local architect.*

158. *A room at the Chequers Inn, Brentwood.*

159. *Socialite and diarist Henry 'Chips' Channon with his son Paul, in 1938 when the family moved into Kelvedon Hall. Painting by James Gunn.*

also knocked down. Burton's the tailors occupied the site from 1939 onwards. Against these losses could be set one gain. St Michael's RC School ended its unhappy occupation of Kelvedon Hall. During its brief (1934-7) occupation one pupil died of tetanus after a playground accident, another of cerebral haemorrhage and a third of pneumonia, while a nun was founded drowned and an elderly pensioner living in the house fell to her death from a third floor window. A week later the Mother Superior closed the school. Kelvedon Hall was bought by the wealthy Anglo-American MP, diarist and socialite Henry 'Chips' Channon (1897-1958), who restored it to its former elegance and added a pair of entrance lodges.

During World War Two the house was used as a convalescent home. Chips Channon bequeathed to his son Paul (1935-), now Lord Kelvedon, both Kelvedon Hall and his parliamentary seat of Southend West. In 1969 the then Roy Strong, youthful director of the National Portrait Gallery, was invited to Kelvedon Hall for the weekend by Paul Channon, then Opposition Spokesman for the Arts. Strong arranged to travel there with fellow guests the Marquess and Marchioness of Dufferin by rail but appears not to have known that the correct station for Kelvedon Hatch is not Kelvedon. Consequently they found themselves "hurtling miles by taxi across country". Notwithstanding this near-disaster, the occasion turned out to be "an idyllic country-house weekend", with "luxury of luxuries ... breakfast in bed with *all* the Sunday newspapers." Strong also commended the Hall as "done over in the best

style by David Hicks". He was back the following year, one of seven hundred and fifty guests who stayed up till dawn to mark the Queen Mother's seventieth birthday.

In 1934 Brentwood's local government jurisdiction was enlarged to include South Weald, Hutton and Ingrave. In the same year the Romford-Shenfield railway was increased from two tracks to four and the Palace cinema was rebuilt. In George V's Jubilee year of 1935 an open air swimming pool was opened in North Road and the year following King George's Playing Fields were created between Ingrave Road and Hartswood Road by Brentwood Urban District Council. 1937 saw the opening of a new Brentwood Police Station and 1938 an Odeon cinema. In the same year, out at West Horndon, what was to become known as Rotary Hoes opened as Howard's Rotavator Co. Ltd.

Facing the Future

UNDER FIRE

In September 1939 alone six thousand London children were evacuated to Brentwood, mostly from Leytonstone and West Ham. The Selo factory switched to large-scale production of film for aerial reconnaissance. The Moat House at Brook Street was taken over by the Sub-Area Quartering Commandant and the army also took over Weald Hall. Kelvedon Hall became a convalescent centre. During the run-up to D-day there were major troop concentrations at Thorndon Park, Weald Park and Childerditch and one carriageway of the A127 was turned into a vast vehicle park.

The first bomb fell at what is now the New World Inn, Great Warley in July 1940, the last on London Road cemetery in April 1944. The first V1 to hit Essex fell in Hill Road on 15 June 1944. The area was to receive seven more, the last in East Horndon in December 1944. The first V2 rocket of seven exploded in Alexander Lane, Shenfield in October 1944, the last hit Hutton Park in March 1945. Brentwood suffered a total of 432 casualties, including 43 dead. By comparison Barking, far more densely built up and a dozen miles closer to central London, was hit by four times as many V-weapons and suffered almost six times as many fatalities.

LOSSES AND GAINS

In the first two post-war decades many historic features disappeared from the locality. Warley Place was demolished, although its grounds were not designated as a nature reserve until 1977. In 1946 the Weald Hall estate was broken up and Weald Hall itself was torn down in 1950. The Bell Inn in Brentwood High Street closed in 1951 and the Yorkshire Grey in 1961. The former George and Dragon Inn on the corner of Crown Street survived until 1970. What was left of Thoby Priory was demolished in 1955 and the old house known as Franks, at 49 High Street, in 1956. During the 1960s Great Stomford Farm House in Hart Street, dating from *c.* 1450 was swept away as were 84/84A High Street, dating from the sixteenth century: their site is now occupied by Café Rouge. A major redevelopment of the King's Road area in 1972 involved the destruction of the Railway Tavern to make way for the building of Ewing

160. *A memorial marks the explosion of a landmine in Navestock churchyard.*

House. In 1975 Rochetts was destroyed by fire and the stables consequently converted into dwellings. At the end of the decade Pegasus House was built on the old goods yard by the station. The Parade by the station went in 1985 so that the Kingsgate office block could occupy its site. The Seven Arches public house in Hartswood Road was demolished in 2000.

With the ending of conscription Warley Barracks were abandoned by the army in 1960. In 1962 the Brook Street toll-house of 1721, having already been moved three times, finally disappeared to make way for the Brentwood by-pass. Robson's Maltings closed that same year and in 1963 Brentwood's Victorian Town Hall went also. In 1964 Wingrave's Forge, which had been in business in Brook Street since 1796, closed at last.

Losses in terms of heritage were offset by gains in population, public amenities and commercial expansion. In 1949 the Shenfield-London line was electrified and between 1952 and 1954 2000 former inhabitants of East Ham were settled on a new housing estate at Ingrave. St Peter's church, Claughton Way, Hutton opened in 1956 to meet the needs of another new housing estate nearby. In 1957 the Queen came to Brentwood to open a new science block at Brentwood School, then celebrating its four hundredth anniversary. Ingatestone's by-pass opened in 1959 but Brentwood had to wait until 1966 to be similarly relieved and Mountnessing until 1973. The M25 opened in 1986.

161. *Tower Arms, South Weald, formerly Jewells – note the importance attached to road access, although the car park is shown empty except for a horse and trap.*

162. *Mountnessing post-mill, re-opened to the public in 1983.*

163. Ingatestone bypass.

Major employers moved in – and out. In 1954 the British Thermos Co. opened in the former City Coach Company headquarters in Ongar Road. The new Ford Motor Company European headquarters opened on the former site of Warley barracks in 1964. Thermos would be gone by the end of the century. Rotary Hoes relocated from Horndon to Suffolk in 1975 and the contracting firm of A E Symes closed its Victoria Works in the Ongar Road in 1978. After eighty years Selo closed its Woodman Road plant at Warley in 1984, with the loss of 1,600 jobs. Between 1981 and 1997 the numbers employed in manufacturing in and around Brentwood fell from 6,600 to 2,700, representing a contraction of almost sixty per cent. Over the same period numbers in the service sector rose from 14,500 to 23,200. Hambro's bank moved into the area in 1976 and Martin Retail Group in 1979. Warley Hill Business Park and a new Territorial Army HQ opened at Warley in 1986. In 1987 Brentwood Enterprise Agency was established to encourage inward investment. The local pattern of employment continued, however, to be dominated by commuting, with almost forty per cent of working residents travelling into London daily and a further fifteen per cent plus travelling elsewhere, mostly to Chelmsford or Basildon. In 1999 British Telecom's flagship headquarters building opened on the site of the former St Faith's hospital. The former Warley Hospital site was simultaneously redeveloped as an up-market residential enclave of more than three hundred homes.

Branches of national retail chains, rather than family-run businesses, began to dominate Brentwood's High Street. In 1954 Rippon's garage was converted into Brentwood Arcade with sixteen shop units. 1955 saw the opening of Tesco at 111 High Street as Brentwood's first self-service store. Fine Fare followed soon after and a Co-op Foodhall in 1959. In 1967 Brentwood's Sainsbury's was built on the site of the former Palace cinema. In 1969 a new Woolworth store opened in Brentwood High Street, though it was subsequently taken over by Marks and Spencer in 1983. Chapel High shopping centre opened in 1975. In 1978 Wilson's Stores finally closed after almost a century as one of Brentwood's local landmarks. In the same year Green's Music and Sports shop, a family business since 1909, also closed down. The Co-op, Brentwood's last department store, went in 1986. Sainsbury's relocated to the former Thermos factory in 1998.

The publication of the *Brentwood Argus* brought a second local newspaper into being in 1968. The expansion of Brentwood's population and commerce necessitated the opening of a new STD telephone exchange in Ongar Road in 1973. Its

164. Quinlan Terry's extension to Brentwood's Roman Catholic cathedral..

14,000 lines represented a huge expansion of capacity compared to the 873 of its 1932 predecessor in Queen's Road.

Recreational opportunities were also expanded. Brentwood's municipal golf course opened at King George's Playing Fields in 1969. In 1973 The Old House in Shenfield Road was opened as an arts centre. In 1983 Mountnessing post-mill opened to the public. In 1987 a new County Library was built in New Road and Brentwood Museum established the following year. The opening of the Brentwood Centre in 1988 made available a first class venue for sports, concerts and entertainment with seating for two thousand. It was complemented by the opening of Brentwood Theatre in Shenfield Road in 1993. In 1995 the formerly secret nuclear bunker at Kelvedon Hatch could be seen by the public. These major gains were offset by minor losses. In 1975 the Odeon cinema closed and in 1980 so did Brentwood's open-air swimming pool.

The growth of population, economy and amenities was matched by a maturing civic pride.

Brentwood Council moved into new neo-Georgian Council Offices in Ingrave Road in 1957; these were further extended in 1984. Brentwood District Council's boundaries were redefined and substantially enlarged in 1974. In 1979 Brentwood was twinned with Landkreis Roth in Bavaria. In 1985 Brentwood, Tennessee became a Sister City and in 1994 a further twinning agreement was signed with Montbazon in France. The completion of Quinlan Terry's Roman Catholic Cathedral in 1991 gave Brentwood an adornment of national importance. In 1993 Brentwood became a borough with Councillor Alf Slaymark as its first mayor. One of the new Brentwood's first acts was to honour the Royal Anglian Regiment with the freedom of entry to the borough. In 1994 Brentwood became the first town in Britain to install colour CCTV. In 2000 the town centre Conservation Area was significantly enlarged. In the same year the Brentwood Town Centre Partnership was created to promote co-operation between local business and the council.

Chronology

1013 Ethelred grants land at Horndon to Sigered
1062 South Weald probably divided from Havering
1067 Manor of Hutton granted to Battle Abbey
1086 Domesday Book
c.1150 South Weald church known to be in existence
1155 Blackmore priory founded
1167-8 Montfichet holding at Fryerning passes to Knights Hospitaller
1176 First recorded reference to Brentwood
1177 Abbey of St Osyth founded
1201 Leper hospital in existence at Brook Street
1221 Probable date for the building of a chapel dedicated to St Thomas Becket
1227 Market known to be in existence
1232 Hubert de Burgh arrested in St Thomas's chapel
Prior and canons of Blackmore granted the right to hold a fair
1327 Lay subsidy returns list 49 South Weald men
1344 Earliest record of a church at Kelvedon Hatch
1381 Poll tax protests spark the Peasants' Revolt
1388 Chantry chapel of St Mary established
Richard II visits Brentwood
1450 Edmund Coningsburgh becomes vicar of South Weald
1523 Lay subsidy returns list 61 names for South Weald
1525 Augustinian priory at Blackmore and Thoby Priory dissolved
1536 Augustinian priory at Mountnessing dissolved
1546 Heresy trials at Brentwood
1555 William Hunter burned for heresy
1557 Brentwood School founded
1561 Elizabeth I visits Ingatestone Hall
1577 Rioting women prevent demolition of St Thomas's chapel
1579 Brentwood Assize House built
1588 Cavalry rally at Brentwood to face expected Spanish invasion
1599 Will Kemp dances through Brentwood
1625 Outbreak of plague
1637 First postmaster known at Brentwood
1638 Charles I passes through Brentwood
1648 Royalist cavalry rendezvous at Brentwood
1664-5 Outbreak of plague
1669 Cosmo III, Grand Duke of Tuscany visits Thorndon Hall
1670 South Weald has 105 houses
1690 Shenfield Place built
1692 William and Mary dine at Ingatestone
1695 First recorded meeting of Brentwood vestry
1696 First turnpike gate in Essex set up at Mountnessing
1707 Congregational church founded

1713 Gentlemen's Club in existence at the White Hart
1719 The Hyde, Fryerning built
1721 Middlesex and Essex Turnpike Trust takes over London-Harwich road
1735 St Nicholas church Ingrave built
1737 Brentwood workhouse established
1738 8th Lord Petre builds St Nicholas' church Ingrave
1742 Warley Common used as a military camp
1752 Tower family acquire control of South Weald
1753 Church of St Nicholas rebuilt at Kelvedon Hatch
1763 Johnson and Boswell pass through Brentwood and Ingatestone
Daniel Sutton opens inoculation house at Fryerning
1764 Mr Arnold opens a Music Assembly Room at Great Warley
Steeple of South Weald church struck by lightning
Building of new Thorndon Hall begins
1770 Navestock Common enclosed
James Paine completes rebuilding of Thorndon Hall
1772 Food riot in Brentwood
1776 Boyles Court rebuilt
1778 George III reviews troops at Warley and visits Thorndon Hall
Enclosure of lands at West Horndon by Lord Petre
1779 "The most dreadful storm that has been known to the oldest man"
1785 London-Norwich mail-coach service inaugurated
1789 Jackson-Inglestone boxing match held at Ingatestone
1801 First census records population of South Weald as 881, Brentwood 1,007
1805 Warley Barracks built
1807 Mountnessing post mill built
1811 Demolition of Navestock Hall
1812 Inclosure Act
1813 Congregational chapel erected in Ingatestone
1833 McAdam upgrades Shenfield-Chelmsford Road
1835 St Thomas's church rebuilt
1836 A hot-air balloon flies over Brentwood
1837 St Helen's chapel consecrated
Great Myles's, Kelvedon Hatch demolished.
1840 Railway station opened at Brentwood
1841 South Weald population 1,450
Brentwood votes to adopt gas-lighting
1842 East India Company purchases Warley Barracks
Brentwood Hall estate sold
1843 Eastern Counties Railway reaches Colchester
1846 Christ Church school built on Warley Hill
1847 Brentwood Congregational Church opened in New Road

1851 Brentwood's first police station opened in Coptfold Road
Population of South Weald 1,383, Brentwood 2,205
Brentwood School and Charity Act passed
1853 Essex Lunatic Asylum opened
1854 Shoreditch Agricultural and Industrial School opened in London Road
Smallpox outbreak
1855 Parish of Christ Church, Warley founded
Burgess and Key, agricultural engineers opened
1857 Board of Health criticizes Brentwood cleansing arrangements
1861 Monument to William Hunter erected
St Helen's school opened
1864 Assize House demolished
Brentwood Town Hall opened
1866 Brentwood water supply laid on
1868 South Weald church restored
1869 Brentwood sewerage system completed
1872 Convent of Mercy established by Canon John Kyne
1873 Brentwood established as a parish
1874 Election riot in Brentwood
London School Board industrial school established
1876-86 Essex County Cricket Club based at Shenfield Road
1877 Last Brentwood Fair held
1878 Thorndon Hall damaged by fire
1881 Church of the Holy Cross opened in Warley
1883 Wilson & Co. opened as boot and shoe retailer
St Thomas's church rebuilt
1884 Brentwood sewerage system upgraded
Committee of Conservators established
1885 Shoreditch Agricultural and Industrial School becomes the Hackney Union Branch Workhouse and Infants' School
1886 Volunteer Drill Hall opened in Ongar Road
Baptist church established in Brentwood
1887 Priory Polo Club established at Hutton Hall
1889 Shenfield station opened
Fryerning amalgamated with Ingatestone
1892 Brentwood Methodist church rebuilt
1895 Avenue of limes planted on Shenfield Common
Dr Quennell rebuilds Brentwood District Hospital
Church of St Nicholas, Kelvedon Hatch rebuilt
1897 George and John Larkin pay for a fountain in Brentwood to mark Queen Victoria's Diamond Jubilee
1899 Brentwood Urban District Council established
Post Office telephone exchange opened
Little Warley golf club founded
1900 Brentwood and District Mechanics Institute founded
Ursuline Convent High School opened

1901 Population of South Weald 5,933, Brentwood 4,932
1902 Fire station opened in Hart Street, Brentwood
1902-4 Church of St Mary the Virgin built to the designs of C H Townsend and Sir William Reynolds Stephens
1904 Ilford photographic factory opens at Great Warley
1905 Royal (later Advance) Laundry opens in Ongar Road
1906 Poplar Training Schools established in Hutton by George Lansbury
Brentwood Operatic Society founded
1909 Wilson's Great Eastern Stores rebuilt after fire
1910 New Brentwood School buildings opened
William Hunter memorial rebuilt
Shen Place Almshouses built
Jean Pierre Hensmans motor business opens in Brook Street
1912 Brook Park estate sold
1913 Brentwood County High School established
1914 Electric Palace opens as Brentwood's first cinema
1915 King's Road Baptist church built
1917 Bomb dropped on Shenfield kills Nurse Evans
Brentwood RC diocese formed
1919 *Brentwood Gazette* established
1920 Local bus services begin
Thorndon Park Golf Club founded
1921 Marillac sanatorium opened
Midland Bank opens in Brentwood High Street
Selo factory re-opens
Brentwood War Memorial erected in Shenfield Road
Marconi telegraph stations built off Ongar Road
1922 Parade cinema, Brentwood opened
Shenfield Memorial Parish Hall opened
1924 Sainsbury's opens in Brentwood High Street
1927 Brentwood County High School for Girls opened
1930 Hackney Union Workhouse becomes St Faith's Hospital
Brentwood's first Woolworth's opens
1931 South Weald population 6,370
1934 Brentwood Urban District Council boundaries enlarged to include South Weald, Hutton and Ingrave
Romford-Shenfield railway increased from two tracks to four
Electric Palace cinema rebuilt as the Palace
1935 Swan Inn rebuilt
Open-air swimming-pool opened in 1936
City Coach Co. established in Ongar Road
King George's Playing Fields opened
Martyr's Elm replaced
1937 New Brentwood police station opens
1938 Odeon cinema opened
Rotary Hoes opened at West Horndon

1939	Chequers inn demolished and Burton's built on the site
1940	Parade cinema closed
	First bomb falls on Great Warley
1944-5	V-bomb attacks
1946	Weald Hall estate broken up
1947	District Cottage Hospital on Shenfield Common becomes the Brentford Maternity Home
1949	Shenfield-London line electrified
1950	Weald Hall demolished
1952	Kelvedon Hatch nuclear bunker built
1952-5	Former East Ham residents resettled at Ingrave
1954	Thermos factory opened
1955	Thoby Priory demolished
1957	Ingrave Road council offices completed
	Queen Elizabeth II opens new science building at Brentwood School
1959	Ingatestone by-pass opened
1960	Warley barracks closed
1961	Yorkshire Grey closed
1962	Brook Street Toll House demolished
1963	Brentwood Town Hall demolished
	Marillac hospital moves into the former Officers' Mess at Warley
1964	Ford Motor Company offices opened at Warley
1966	Brentwood by-pass opened
1967	Nuffield Nursing Home in Shenfield Road built
1968	Palace cinema closed
	Brentwood Argus established
1973	Arts and Community Centre opens in The Old House, Shenfield Road
	Anglo-European School opened at Ingatestone
1974	Brentwood District redefined
1975	Rotary Hoes leaves Horndon
	Chapel High shopping centre opened
1977	Warley Place becomes a nature reserve
1978	Wilson's Store closed and re-opened as Cooper's
	A E Symes engineering closes Ongar Road site
	Burton's the tailors abandons High Street site
1979	Brentwood twinned with Landkreis Roth, Germany

	Phase I of residential renovation of Thorndon Hall completed
1980	St Faith's Hospital closed
	Open-air swimming-pool closed
1982	Brentwood Theatre Trust formed
1983	Mountnessing post-mill reopened to the public
	Marks & Spencer occupy former Woolworth store in Brentwood High St
1984	Closure of Selo/Ilford plant at Woodman Road
1985	Brentwood becomes sister city of Brentwood, Tennessee
	Parade cinema demolished
1986	Warley Hill Business Park opened
	New Territorial Army HQ opened at Warley
	M25 opened
1987	New Brentwood library built in New Road
	Brentwood Enterprise Agency established
1988	Brentwood Centre, Doddinghurst Road opened
	Advance Laundry, Ongar Road closed
1991	Roman Catholic cathedral of St. Mary and St. Helen dedicated
1993	Brentwood acquires Borough status
	Brentwood Theatre opened in Shenfield Road
1994	Brentwood twinned with Montbazon, France
	Brentwood becomes the first British town to install colour CCTV
	St George's church, Ongar Road completed
1995	Kelvedon Hatch nuclear bunker opened to the public
1997	St Faith's Hospital demolished
1998	New Brentwood Sainsbury's store opened
1999	British Telecom building completed
	Black Horse, Pilgrim's Hatch damaged by fire
	Redevelopment of Warley Hospital site for housing
	Anglia Polytechnic University leaves Brentwood
2000	Brentwood Town Centre Conservation Area extended
	Brentwood Town Centre Partnership formed
	Black Horse, Pilgrims' Hatch restored and reopened

Further Reading

(ERO = Essex Record Office)

William Addison: *Essex Worthies* (Phillimore 1973)

John Booker: *Essex and the Industrial Revolution* (ERO 1974)

A F J Brown: *Essex at Work 1700-1815* (ERO 1969)

A F J Brown: *Essex People 1750-1900* (ERO 1972)

A F J Brown: *Prosperity and Poverty: Rural Essex 1700-1815* (ERO 1996)

C Butler: *Ingrebourne and other poems* (WB Whittingham & Co. 1884)

Sir George Clutton: *Old Thorndon Hall, Essex: a history and reconstruction of its park and garden* (Garden History Society Occasional Papers No. 2 1970)

D Defoe: *Tour through the Eastern Counties*

A C Edwards: *John Petre; essays on the life and background of John, 1st Lord Petre 1549-1613* (Regency Press 1975)

F G Emmison: *Elizabethan Life: Essex Gentry Wills* (ERO 1978)

F G Emmison: *Elizabethan Life: Wills of Essex Gentry and Yeomen* (ERO 1980)

F G Emmison: *Elizabethan Life: Home Work and Land* (ERO 1976)

F G Emmison: *Elizabethan Life: Morals and the Church Courts* (ERO 1973)

F G Emmison: *Elizabethan Life: Disorder* (ERO 1970)

Gordon R Everson: *East and West Horndon: A View of the Parish and its Surrounds Today and Yesterday* (Wednesday Press 2001)

John Fryer: *Brentwood: A Concise Pictorial History* (Brentwood Town Centre Partnership 2001)

D I Gordon: *Regional History of Railways of Great Britain: The eastern counties* (David & Charles 1968)

R J Hercock and G A Jones: *Silver by the Ton: A History of Ilford Limited 1879-1979* (McGraw-Hill 1979)

John Hunter: *The Essex Landscape* (ERO 1999)

S M Jarvis and C T Harrison: *In search of Essex: a traveller's companion to the county* (Essex Countryside 1969)

S M Jarvis: *Victorian and Edwardian Essex from old photographs* (Batsford 1973)

Peter Kurton: *Doddinghurst: A Place in the Country* (PBK Publishing 1999)

C T Kuypers *Thorndon: its History and associations* (Brentwood Diocesan Magazine 1930)

Lésley Lewis: *The Private Life of a Country House 1912-39* (David & Charles 1980)

R R Lewis: *William Hunter: An account of his death* (Brentwood School 1955)

R R Lewis *Guide to an exhibition to illustrate the history of Brentwood School 1957* (Brentwood School 1957)

R R Lewis: *Four Hundred Years: the History of Brentwood School* (Governors of Sir Antony Browne's School 1981)

A Le Lievre: *Miss Willmott of Warley Place* (Faber 1980)

Peter C R Linnecar: *Fireside Talks about Brentwood* (J W Larkin 1906)

Peter C R Linnecar: *More Fireside Talks about Brentwood* (J W Larkin 1920) (Sharon 1989)

George Lloyd: *The Place at Brook Street: A history of Marygreen Manor Hotel* (Marygreen Books 1997)

M G Mckerness: *Brentwood County High School 1913-63* (Brentwood Press 1964)

John Marriage: *Bygone Brentwood* (Phillimore 1990)

A Stuart Mason: *Essex on the Map: The 18th century Land Surveyors of Essex* (ERO 1990)

W F Quin: *Brentwood Congregational Church: a brief history 1672-1972* (The Author 1972)

N Scarfe: *Essex* (Faber 1975)

Charles Sale: *Korty: The Legend Explained* (Ian Henry 1986)

Frank D Simpson: *Brentwood in old picture postcards* (European Library 1985, 2 vols)

P Snell: *City in Focus: The City Coach Company an illustrated history* (South Anglia 1991)

Survey of Ingatestone High Street (Ingatestone and Fryerning Historical Society 1989)

Victoria County History of Essex Volume VIII (Oxford University Press 1983)

Gladys A Ward: *A History of South Weald and Brentwood* (G A Ward 1961)

Gladys A Ward: *Victorian and Edwardian Brentwood* (Two Tree Island Press 1980)

J C Ward, K Marshall, I G Roberston: *Old Thorndon Hall* (ERO 1972)

J G S Ward: *A history of the St Thomas of Canterbury Church of England Schools* (The Spire 1967)

William White: *County of Essex* (1845)

E E Wilde and A M Christy: *Ingatestone and the Essex Great Road with Fryerning* (OUP 1913)

Michael Willis and Godfrey Thomas: *Brentwood School: Portrait of a Grammar School and its town* (Governors of Sir Anthony Browne's School 1985)

John Wolters and Kerry Stephenson: *The best of days? memories of Brentwood School* (Brentwood School 1999)

Ian Yearsley: *Ingatestone and Fryerning: a history* (Ian Henry Publications 1997)

ARTICLES

Essex Journal

G Caunt: 'Lord St.Vincent at Rochetts' (VIII 1973)

G A Ward: 'A Brentwood Surgeon: Cornelius Butler 1789-1871' (II 1967)

Essex Review

J L Cranmer-Byng: 'Essex prepares for invasion' (LIX LX LXI 1950-2)

E P Dickin: 'Provision for Guests and Horses in Essex' (LIII 1944)

F G Emmison: '1555 and all that: a milestone in the History of the English Road' (LXIV 1955)

K A Frost: 'Electrification in Suburban Essex' (LIII 1944)

G O Rickword: 'The Crown Inn, Brentwood' (LV 1946)

G A Ward: 'Recollections of an Old Soldier of John Company' (LV 1946)

Index

Asterisks denote illustration
or caption